Cheddar Gorged

Milk, culture, rennet, and salt,

This is the ingredient list default.

Bring these together and you have a cheese,

An alchemist's mix of many degrees.

Warm up the milk, add a cultural heart,

The rennet solidifies, the knife slides apart.

The curd swims free, releasing its whey,

And salt preserves the curd

for another day.

. . . .

SEAN WILSON

GREAT NORTHERN

ACKNOWLEDGEMENTS

To Carol for giving me the love and drive to push on with this book

To David Burrill, my publisher, for believing in me

To Steven Lloyd for bringing David and me together

To my sadly missed grandparents Frank and Mona, who helped me to believe in myself and all that is good

To all at Wyke Farms for their support thus far

To Nigel (the nose) Pooley for his Foreword

To James Montgomery for his hospitality and support

To Geoff Lloyd for his fabulous photography
www.geofflloydphotography.co.uk

To my informal editors – Colin David, Lesley Churm – who got me off to a great start

To my formal editor – Ross Jamieson – who made sure we had an excellent finish

To our grateful neighbours for taste-testing these recipes!

To all my cheesemeister followers for your continued support

All the specialist cheese-sellers who work tirelessly to bring you the best in class – every time

And finally, thanks to you for picking up my book – let's Gorge on Cheddar!

Great Northern Books
PO Box 1380, Bradford, BD5 5FB
www.greatnorthernbooks.co.uk

© Sean Wilson 2022

ISBN: 978-1-914227-28-8

Design and layout: David Burrill

CIP Data
A catalogue for this book is available from the British Library

. . .

The heart beats fast and acidities rise,
One wrong move now and you're in for a surprise.
Add the rennet quick to help calm that progression,
The cutters will make a timely impression.
Splitting the curd to a suitable size,
Thousands of cubes, the cheese-maker's prize,
For understanding and watching and measuring skill,
There's just one thing now, the salt, two jobs to fill
To bring out the flavour and to harness the time,
Making our cheese somewhere near sublime.

From milk to mature with these four ingredients
Tempered in youth and taught to be obedient
To flourish through life and improve with good age
Becoming vintage is where a cheese will engage.

Bringing the herd's milk out of the alchemist's mist,
A daily chore that cannot be missed.
Preserving life's milk lactated for us,
To mother and nurture and mature and thus,
Bring forth beautiful food from a cheese-maker's strife,
The four stages of cheese, matching the four stages of life.

CONTENTS

FOREWORD

What an inspired name – *Cheddar Gorged* for everything good and inspiring about our nation's, and even the world's, favourite cheese.

I am Nigel Pooley, a person with dairy running through me from head to toe, having spent almost fifty-nine years working in the production side of the dairy industry and having just retired in January 2022. During this time I have seen so many changes and I have to say all for the good and improvement of the dairy products we eat and love, and in particular Cheddar cheese. I started my dairy life at the now famous Cheddar Cheese Dairy at Davidstow in Cornwall, ended at Wyke Farms in Somerset, and in between covered production of most dairy products and all aspects of dairy management.

I had known of Sean Wilson, but only as Martin Platt in *Coronation Street* where he had been a prominent face for over twenty years.

I first met Sean in September 2009 when we were both guests on *The Alan Titchmarsh Show* on BBC One. It was a show with a cheese theme. I had just had my nose insured for £5 million as a cheese grader and selector with an exceptional sense of smell and taste, while Sean had just launched his new company, the Artisan Farm Cheese Company, handmaking regional Lancashire cheese as a fully fledged cheesemaker. Also on the show was Jody Scheckter, the former Formula One racing champion and now owner of the largest buffalo herd in Europe and making superb mozzarella at Laverstoke Farm in Hampshire.

We continued our friendship at cheese shows and other cheesy events. Often we would both be judging cheese or Sean would be the celebrity guest at either the Frome or the Mid-Somerset cheese shows, of which I was the chairman. Sean would normally enter some of his own handcrafted Lancashire cheese and be like an expectant father as the results were revealed, and so pleased when he won an award.

Sean, with his acting background, soon became the media face of cheese and often appeared on national TV whenever a cheese story broke. Even now he is a great ambassador for all UK cheeses, and in particular his favourite Lancashire.

He has chosen to write about Cheddar firstly because of its all-round popularity and versatility. Sean is also an accomplished cook, having worked in a Michelin-star restaurant, and so was keen to showcase this by cooking a wide range of recipes featuring Cheddar cheese. This book contains over sixty recipes, each using Cheddar cheese, and are so varied you will not believe until you read and try them for yourself. In this book Sean is keen to portray the history of Cheddar cheese and the changes in quality and flavour over time, and to educate us all on the important factors and the key things which have made the biggest differences. The biggest focus for all cheesemakers today is the consumer, which is why quality in terms of flavour and texture are all-important, so that the customer knows that the cheese they buy this week will be the same as that bought last week.

I am sure that you will find this book informative and interesting from an inspirational man who is an actor, cook, cheesemaker, a very accomplished painter, and who I am proud to call a friend.

Nigel Pooley
April 2022

The passions that build up our human soul,
Not with the mean and vulgar works of man,
But with high objects, with enduring things,
With life and nature, purifying thus
The elements of feeling and of thought,
And sanctifying, by such discipline,
Both pain and fear, until we recognise
A grandeur in the beatings of the heart.

from *The Prelude* by William Wordsworth

CHEDDAR GORGED

If like me, you dream of a better world,
A compassionate and more forgiving world,
A world where culture has a profound and uplifting effect on you,
Witnessing the magic of milk being fashioned by a craftsman/woman
into an artisan cheese,
The nuance of European wine culture, the importance of
terroir and provenance,
Then you will have the same artistic human drive I have, to seek out
the 'great' in the world.

Great: An object, a craft, a culture, a moment in time, a taste. Something as simple as a sip, a distant whiff, a sound. A moment that has a story, a history through human intellectual learning. To eventually burst forth to reveal a masterpiece.

A giant deep within awakens when it realises the importance of culture the world has to offer. We all have a passion and it will reveal itself when we quietly love something. Cheese can be one such special love and I am looking to thread this passion through the pages of this book.

A PASSION FOR FOOD

At its best, cheese is alchemy, it is magic. It has a direct connection with the past, where the knowledge of humankind collides with the natural world to create a palate supernova.

MY EARLY LOVE AFFAIR WITH CHEESE

Once we leave the education system with a skill for learning, and with at least eleven years of classroom antics under our belts, we are then released from the pen into the world and all it has to offer, and at some point the true realisation of culture will come to us. We will sing out loud a favourite chorus or cry to a poem or experience an intense stimulation from a simple mouthful of food.

This is culture and passion.

This is my better world.

It is a security blanket of adulthood that lets me focus on the important stuff, where each step forward feeds my cultural yearning – and where this yearning then yearns some more for the next experience. It is a space to learn, my new classroom, where I am both student and teacher, and I recognise

'A grandeur in the beatings of the heart.'

There is a word derived from the French that might be of interest here: *Gourmandise*. It means the love of good food, but more so the psycho-physiology of food, of eating, of the effects of good food cooked well, whether that be jugged hare or a quick salad. The cooking of food and the thought of eating it cultivate in us a physiological effect and a chain of motor events that lead to our producing gastric juices. Food hurriedly snatched to refuel is one thing; but a considered and wholesome meal delivered to the table, a joy to smell from the moment you walk in through the front door, is something else altogether. The former has a detrimental effect on us and only satisfies a need; and so the body hasn't time to consider the digestion of the snack, and cannot prepare itself physiologically. The latter, however, satisfies from within, it digests well, and the body thanks you with a calm and sated purr of satisfaction.

No doubt all of us are familiar with both scenarios. We recognise the bloated discomfort when we don't prepare our bodies to eat, but hopefully we have all looked forward to a meal in lovely, relaxed surroundings too, and have felt the comfort of good digestion. In the long run, it is better for us to prepare our bodies. The benefits to our well-being and digestion will be worthwhile and impressive. We will be happier, our moods much improved, and our days will be more enjoyable. Of course, many things in our day-to-day lives get in the way of good digestion. Stress is a huge factor here. But by taking on positive, effective eating habits you can cut the levels of stress your body suffers by half. Take the working Frenchman. At lunchtime he will park up his van, erect a foldaway table, and sit down to enjoy his lunch. It is deeply ingrained in the European culture.

A Frenchman doesn't live to work; he works to live.

This is Gourmandise.

There is much to be learned here. I urge us all to allow ourselves to let it into our lives, at least occasionally. Do so, and keep an eye on your mood. It will become obvious which of the two scenarios is more beneficial to a happier life.

For me this is a lifelong learning curve. Sometimes a simple visit to a little restaurant in a new town has sparked a desire to cook locally, with local ingredients, and with local chefs. Sometimes I have discovered an epicurean book to dive into, and which has stirred a slow but sure understanding that this food culture really does exist.

MY LEARNING CURVE

I guess it all began back in my late teens when I watched the charismatic Keith Floyd on his jaunts around France. I was really into my cooking, the flavours were brand new and the fusion of unlikely ingredients was exciting. It reminded me of the way a colour wheel shows an artist the relationship between colours, but for a different sense – taste. A flavour wheel, if you like. But it was about more than that too. There was a whole culture caught up in the produce, the recipes, the dishes. For me it was a point of arrival and I was ready to learn.

It was the 1980s and I was travelling through Burgundy, consumed with a passion for food and an appetite to broaden my knowledge. After a lovely home-cooked meal at a chateau in Morey-Saint-Denis, the owner, a puffed-up, haughty Frenchwoman, slid a small cheese in front of me. I frowned, but she sternly handed me a spoon and with a Gallic gesture encouraged me to tackle the fromage. I pushed the spoon through the orange-hued skin, then further into the soft centre of the cheese. It transported me to somewhere new, but also somewhere confusing. English cheese was mostly hard – Cheddar, Red Leicester, Gloucester – the softest a Somerset Brie. So, under the moody gaze of my host, I pulled the spoon from the soft centre and sniffed the cheese. It smelled of farm, of a herd of cattle crossing the farmyard cobbles. Tentatively, I bit into it and was met with a savoury sweetness as my tongue pushed the melting paste around my palate, a depth of flavours unfolding: of freshly mown grass, of mushrooms, and with a lovely buttery finish. What an experience!

I discovered it was a washed-rind cheese, washed with Marc de Bourgogne, a harsh brandy from the third pressing of the grape. The name of the cheese was Ami du Chambertin and it had been turned and washed every day by hand for a month. What commitment!

The experience not only sparked my love affair with great and complex cheese, but my gastronomic maturity grew from here. I began to take seriously the world of the 'epicurean' and discovered the meaning of 'provenance':

PROVENANCE

/ˈprov(ə)nans

Noun: The place of origin or earliest known history of something;

Where a food meets its own history and where the food is then made at its actual source;

From the French word Provenir, 'to come from'.

Provenance helps food producers to add value, quality and broader social benefits to their products. Under transportation, milk has been found to lose some of its creamy qualities. So, the less the milk travels, the greater the chances of producing an outstanding cheese. Consumers often want to contribute to the local economy, and so the relationship between local producers and consumers encourages a shared knowledge of a regional product and a connection to taste, location and community.

THE HISTORY OF CHEDDAR

All sorts of different food types have been a part of our diet for hundreds of years. They all have fascinating stories to tell, each with its own origin and cultural contribution. Cheddar is one such food; and, since we will be gorging on all things Cheddar, we should explore its history, from its humble beginnings to its dominance as the nation's go-to cheese.

Today, like many traditional products, Cheddar cheese exists within a cultural tension between its original production methods and a very modern industrial machine aimed at profit margins and volume. Cheddar is a commodity and a global phenomenon, so the complexities of market forces are always there. Of course, Cheddar has much to be grateful for in the world's supermarket system and should be applauded for the mountains of cheese produced and circulated to keep up with rising demand.

It is a tricky balance to sustain. On the one hand, it is essential to satisfy the need for mass production, to supply supermarket shelves with units of classic taste, and to impress the eye with packaging that carries the message of the producer's proud integrity and authenticity. But on the other hand, cheesemakers craft a proud and traditional product, and therefore long-cherished family recipes and techniques must be upheld.

But how much do we really know about the history of the nation's favourite cheese? We have to step back in time to the village of Cheddar in Somerset in 1170 AD to find the first written record of cheesemaking in the region. However, this wasn't the first British cheese to be recorded. That legend goes back nearly a thousand years, to Cheshire in 1082. Common sense suggests that, due to a lack of recordkeeping and literacy in the farming community, medieval farmers had been using excess milk to make these cheeses long before records began. In cultural terms it is a deep-time tradition: cheeses were named after the places in which they were produced, and our indigenous cheeses are still named this way today.

But back then life was an altogether different prospect. The deadly onslaught of leprosy was rampant and for centuries Glastonbury Abbey and secular buildings housed many of the unfortunates; wolves roamed forested regions, including Somerset, and were a daily threat to humans and their livestock; and waves of Norman and Viking invaders brutally laid claim to the Isles. Life was fraught with menacing threats. It was a frugal and pagan existence, and, safe to say, the need for food only satisfied a basic need for nourishment and survival.

The task of cheesemaking rested with the womenfolk at the 300 or so farms across the Somerset and Dorset region. The cheese was only distributed locally to the farming workforce and the immediate community. But the inability to record any exact recipes, as well as the variable standards of cheesemaking equipment, must have resulted in the fractured and inconsistent evolution of cheese production in the Cheddar area.

As time passed and techniques and equipment improved, the number of cheesemaking dairies increased and fed into farmers' entrepreneurial desires to make more money from their milk yield. Cheddar was being produced across the seasons of spring, summer and autumn, but not winter. These fine-weather cheeses were an important development in south-western farming because the preserving of milk quotas into cheese enabled farmers to nourish the community with a much-needed means for surviving the harsh winter months.

Elsewhere, cheese produced and sold by the Home Counties to the London market was blighted by London negotiants who complained that the cheese had soured or was no longer consumable after transportation. Such complaints were widely fabricated and attracted underhand sales tactics. The farming community grew wary of conducting business with the capital, and so

Cheddar cheese was generally only available in Somerset, Dorset and Wiltshire.

Cheesemaking was now up and running in earnest, and an inevitable competitive edge crept into the game, whereby every Cheddar dairy aspired to produce the most sought-after cheese in the district. A little competition may well have been healthy for furthering producers' knowledge, but no two farms' cheeses were alike. The cheeses were indeed made in Cheddar, but Cheddar cheese didn't really exist yet. There were huge variations in flavour and craftmanship. Cheesemaking is a science and, as such, needed to be understood in scientific terms before there was any chance of creating a standard, representative Cheddar.

CAVE AGING

However, there was some light shining through the darkness, in the shape of the 147-metre-high natural caves in the environs of Cheddar. The caves were formed from limestone strata developed over millennia, creating the striking, world-famous Cheddar Gorge on the southern edge of the Mendip Hills. The locals found that the caves' near-constant temperature of 12°C and their perfect humidity were ideal conditions for aging cheese for up to twelve months, or even longer. In my mind, this 'cave aging' was a happy accident: the caves refrigerated and matured the cheese, but ultimately they protected it.

This remarkable technique shouldn't be downplayed. The cave aging of Parmesan was not recorded until the 16th century, although Roquefort is mentioned in the ancient records at the monastery of Conques in France in 1070 AD, and cave-aged Gorgonzola dates back to 879 AD. So, all pretty much around the same time as Cheddar and there is some doubt whether the Gorgonzola method could have travelled to Somerset by then. Nonetheless, cave aging was a significant factor in the success story of the early development of Cheddar cheese.

The cheese emanating from Cheddar at the time, although of a random nature and not a cheese of distinction in the modern sense, was said to be earthy and complex. It was soon in demand and much talked of in higher circles. In 1170, King Henry II, known for his 'good living', ordered an unprecedented batch from the Mendip caves. He bought 10,240 lbs (4.6 tons) of the cave-aged Cheddar at a farthing per lb (£10.60, which in modern money amounts to £25,600) and had it shipped to London to sit proud on the banqueting tables of the royal court. It soon became the Plantagenet 'must-have' among the upper classes, the capital's de rigueur, go-to cheese.

This single sale of Cheddar cheese bore witness to the birth of Somerset's shining star.

ACT I OF THE MODERN CHEDDAR:
THE UNIFYING OF A 'DEFINITE' CHEDDAR RECIPE

So cheesemaking in Somerset and Dorset continued its erratic progress for some time, and I guess the development of flavour and quality was slow and very much hit and miss. Many cheesemakers were involved in the quest for Cheddar quality, but one individual stands out, with his place at the head of the table, as the *Father of Cheddar Cheese*.

Enter stage left, Joseph Harding. Born in 1805, he was the second of seven children to the Yeoman-Harding family of Marksbury, Somerset. The family history was of Wiltshire stock and Joseph had five generations of dairy and cheesemaking heritage to fall back on. A well-respected family in the region, one ancestor was a groom to Charles II and elected a Member of Parliament in 1640.

Joseph intended to bring about a unified recipe for a cheese to represent the region in a more understandable and joined up way, and to create a more reliable longevity for any cheese produced in a cleaner environment. Concerned by the hygiene of cheesemaking methods, he was keen to study and clean up the process. He was insistent on absolute cleanliness and the milkers were not allowed to bring milk in 'direct from the field'. They had to pour it into a receiver outside the dairy wall,

'Whence by means of a pipe it was conveyed inside to the cheese tub. Thus being conveyed by a conduit, at each end of which a strainer be placed to prevent any filth from the yard from passing into the cheese-tub'. Joseph had discovered 'an easy way of draining the curds of as much of their moisture as possible'. This resulted in a semi-hard, close-textured, non-crumbly cheese. He had created the universally regarded style associated with Cheddar.

His dictum: 'Cheese is not made in the field, nor in the byre, nor even in the cow, it is made in the dairy.'

His idea of a good Cheddar cheese was, 'close in texture, yet mellow in character or quality; it is rich with a tendency to melt in the mouth, the flavour full and fine, approaching to that of the hazelnut.'

From this point on, the method became known as the 'Definite Formula'. The rules of cleanliness were attributed to Joseph, but his modifying the methods for timing, temperature and acidity all helped to create a recipe of consistently good cheese. Such techniques were major developments in food hygiene.

Furthermore, Joseph continued to improve his methods by insisting that a 'sharp cutting instrument in breaking the curd is injurious and that the curd should be allowed to split apart according to its natural grain'. He went on to invent the automatic curd cutter, 'the revolving breaker', and in turn economised the human effort required to make cheese.

The more correct method of 'Cheddaring' would have worked better. To explain, Cheddaring is the process of cutting, turning and stacking the curds on top of each other, to expel moisture and to allow them to 'knit' together. If you were to look at the curd from a side angle, they would look like the pages of a book. Layering curds in this manner has the effect of 'pushing' out excess moisture through the gentle force of gravity.

In later years, the revolving breaker was considered a flawed technique as it caused too much damage to the curd. So, back came Cheddaring for some of the cheese fraternity. Cheddaring is still used in Farmhouse production today where there isn't the urgency of cheese production. Farmhouse Cheddar-making has the benefit of being a calmer and more time-friendly form of cheesemaking.

SPREADING THE WORD, GLOBALLY

Joseph was a religious man with a firm moral compass. He and his wife, Rachel Harding, advocated education and therefore proposed the establishment of the Somerset Agriculture College, which they believed was a suitable venue for their teachings. The Hardings offered their knowledge free of charge. Their new method of consistent Cheddar-making was having an impact and spreading through the land. They both taught north of the border in Scotland, passing on their Cheddar-making methods, which would account for the quality of Scottish Cheddar-making today.

They received visits from Americans who took their ideas back across the Atlantic to eventually set up mass production in New York, way before the UK ever considered it. Joseph even sent his son to Australia to spread the word of Cheddar-making. It was the ultimate sacrifice, in the search for a unity of spirit, in the name of adventure, because he never saw his son again. Indeed, the whole family travelled to most continents to give away the secret.

UBIQUITY, MY LOVER

Cheddar cheese; Ubiquity is my middle name
Pick me up in Alaska, New Guinea and Spain
Whether you like it sharp, mild or plain
You'll always remember my name
Like the water in Majorca, flows off the tongue
On a sandwich you bought or on a ploughman's – what can go wrong?
Only the best makes it to my table
Because I have the knowledge and am able
To see, taste and smell – and conjure with fabled
West Country heaven – it's my absolute must
Or my fridge will internally combust
Never let Cheddar from West Country valleys and vales
Made with a method from historic tales
Creamy and sharp and nutty to boot
Sit there in the gloom next to old and slimy bean shoots
Make it the star of myriad meals
It's always there on shelves within some multiple deal
Sit it on top or within a meal, fit for king
It's a ubiquitous, global phenomena thing
So next time you want to just lean in the cooler
For something to sit on that special pork pie from Kent
Pick up that ubiquitous Cheddar – what could be drooler
Than cheese from the caves, sharp and keen – heaven and ubiquity sent.

Sean Wilson, 2022

So, our Cheddar has come a long way, from gruel to feed the pagan workers in the fields, to a clean and well-regarded recipe with a reputation for multi-layered, savoury, deep flavours. Fashioned overseas on the Australian and American continents, it's fair to say that Cheddar was in a productive place and looking forward to a charmed life. Somerset cheese was carrying the status of a cheese of some distinction and was ready to carry forward into global food history. It was blessed with the fabulous fortunes of both alchemy and luck, two of the most important ingredients in a great cheese. From the epicurean point of view, Cheddar had the required integrity, with a quality backstory.

If only it could remain this good.

ACT II OF THE MODERN CHEDDAR:
THE DIFFICULTIES OF THE 20TH CENTURY

Here we have the makings of the multi-twisting narrative of a Dickensian novel. It is a story where our hero, Cheddar, has tiptoed its way through infancy and has stumbled into its teenage years, where it meets a great Svengali, who takes it upon himself to guide the cheese towards a prosperous adult life.

But as with all 'great' foods, what its early producers failed to account for was that it would become the UK's finest and proudest of cheeses, the cheese that would most suit the public's palate, with the versatility to earn its place in the nation's larders. That is, it would still be loved 800 years after it took its first unsteady steps.

Therein lies the most important part of the Cheddar story.

So, what could possibly go wrong? The stage had been set and the historic lineage looked perfect for a quality and economical product to feed the country and provide plenty of vital vitamins and fortifying calcium. Surely Cheddar's future looked rosy, its supremacy assured.

Alas, over time, the winds of change challenged the wherewithal of dairy farmers and cheesemakers up and down the country. There had been the Industrial Revolution; a generation of Victorian entrepreneurs had churned out cotton, iron and foods for huge profits; and steam had been around for some time as the catalyst for mass production. Then the 20th century unleashed a lethal chain of events that would prove astonishing and where the cheese industry would clash head-to-head with the government. The war effort was all-encompassing and Cheddar found itself suffering from the worst imaginable of all threats: the total closure of all Cheddar-making farms, and therefore the extinction of Cheddar cheese itself.

Where the cheesemaker and the farmer, relying on the popularity of their product over centuries, had steered their lives and generations into the trade and cut their cloth accordingly, sadly the farmer would suffer immeasurable damage and be taken to the brink in both monetary and emotional terms.

The 20th century started with a substantial amount of cheese being made up and down the UK. There were 3,500 farms churning out farmhouse cheese, but by the end of the Second World War only 100 were still doing so. The political strife after the First World War brought significant changes and the result was that no cheese was being produced at all. Most farmers decided not to make cheese again, and those farmers that did encountered significant struggles.

Due to the production of milk exceeding demand in the 1920s, cheesemaking to help feed the war-torn social classes and to satisfy the market up to the 1930s was uneconomical. Prices fell and many farms were forced to close.

Most farmers made the decision to withdraw their interests in cheese production and looked elsewhere for profits. I guess feeding the nation with vegetables was more accepted and would at the very least supply some profit. Times were not good and social oppression from the First World War still prevailed, leaving a shell-shocked nation to pick up the pieces of national identity. But with too much milk and an ailing nation trying to get back on its feet, there was in fact an opportunity there for the taking. The government, amid its rhetoric for rebuilding the nation, decided to make a move.

In 1932, it set up a commission to investigate the dairy industry. It was decided there was an urgent need for an organisation to stabilise the market. They deemed it vital to initiate the Agricultural Marketing Act of 1933, to control milk production and its subsequent distribution in the United Kingdom. The manifesto of the newly formed Milk Marketing Board (MMB) was to buy, advertise and sell milk; to guarantee a constant and reasonable price for farmers and find buyers for every drop of milk produced in the UK. This was to be put in place immediately. So, after all the mistrust and price-chipping of the past, where farmers had questioned their very existence, they now found themselves with a future. They now had a lifeline to sell their milk on a fair and daily basis.

As a cooperative, it was the largest agricultural model of its kind in British history. Funded and run by farmers, the MMB encompassed every dairy farm and milk producer in the country, as well as acting as a contact between producers and buyers. The MMB had a two-tier pricing system: farmers were paid more for milk that was going to be sold as liquid, and less for milk that was going into cheese production. Month by month an average price was set and every farmer received a cheque.

Right here is where the story changes for the milk farmers. But the cheesemaking community had issues.

It seemed all was well with the milk community, and it was with the dairy farms; all was good. But the price of milk for cheesemaking was to be sold for less than the liquid milk. Of course dairy farmers wanted the better price for their milk and so the cheesemaker lost out. When you consider the equation of buying milk, making cheese, maturing cheese for months on end, there was a lot of money tied up in that milk and not many farmers had the wherewithal to fund it. Hence there were only 100 cheesemaking dairies able to keep their businesses afloat.

For six years there was unity between the government's will and the liquid milk farming community. The MMB kept their word and the nation was being fed good wholesome milk – at the right price. In the aftermath of closures and family trauma, the farmers were able to feed their families.

So, just twenty-one years after the conclusion of the First World War, the rise of Hitler and the devastating turmoil of Nazism throughout Europe led to the realisation that imports from overseas were somewhere near impossible and so the British government had to find another way to feed the nation. There came, very abruptly, a need for self-sufficiency. The MMB was called into action and utilised the current status quo with a momentous, historic decision: to create a 'Government Cheddar' – a mild Cheddar to be the only cheese made in the UK for the consumption of the nation as part of its war ration quota. It was included in government films and shown in cinemas to promote the eating of government Cheddar instead of meat. Times must have been hard! The Ministry of Information created a number of short 'propaganda' films during the Second World War to keep people informed, because back then for many people their only source of news came from cinemas. Cheddar was used to help keep up the nation's morale. There were slogans, such as:

– Cheese is an excellent body-builder.
– It provides a guard against infections.
– It will help you to see in the dark.
– It's a concentrated energy-giving food.

The films referred to leading experts, who said, 'A piece of Cheddar weighing 5oz gives as much nourishment as a piece of meat weighing 10oz.' Following years of mistrust from farmers and the subsequent effects of driving down price quotas, which resulted in some desperate farmers taking their own lives, all of a sudden Cheddar became a household morale booster, a significant part of the country's war effort.

What a metamorphosis in fortunes that was, albeit in the face of an all-out war, for our south-western cheese. A rise to stardom, from the near death knell of misfortune, was some turnaround for any food or business associated with it. But the remaining 100 creameries were soon inundated with orders for this 'single-recipe mild Cheddar', an impossible quota for so few dairies. So any further needs to satisfy the national requirement for ration volumes was imported from foreign allies.

The MMB was met with firm resistance from the depleted but strong cheesemaking community, who wanted to continue making their Cheshires, their Lancashires, their Wensleydales, in the name of heritage; a heritage built up over nearly a thousand years. I suppose the paranoia was, 'If we start making Cheddar, we will always be making Cheddar.' It was an understandable position to take. In the past they had had to show a similar dogged determination to conserve their territorial, heritage cheeses. There were only 100 dairies, but if they stood firm they were strong.

In the government's eyes this was militancy and they viewed it with disdain. Some dairies seemed to be looking at the war effort with tunnel vision and agreed to make Cheddar at the Ministry of Food's will. Eventually, in January 1943, after much back-and-forth infighting, there were fifty-two closure notices issued by the ministry, of which thirty-five related to the North West region and fourteen in the East Midlands.

Although these 'militant' dairies stood strong and lost out, their determination stood the test of time and, thanks to that doggedness, they still exist today and are fully operational, making fine British territorial cheeses of Stilton, Lancashire and Wensleydale.

It was decreed that 1oz of Cheddar would be made available for any one ration ticket per week. The end suppliers were complaining though, that cutting one ounce of cheese was near impossible. The decision had to be revised and the butchers, grocers and so on were told to serve four weeks' worth of Cheddar to each ticket holder.

The making of Government Cheddar continued until the end of rationing, nine years after the end of the war, in 1954.

So, in real terms, from a position of desperate weakness and human loss due to market forces and untold pressure laid on the farming community in the 1920s, we had the government acting as very unexpected benefactors to the remaining cheese creameries and the liquid milk industry. This relationship went from strength to strength, not least because the community knew the real cost of the alternative and, subsequently, worked hard to create some semblance of normal family life again on their farmsteads.

The MMB had an advertising budget of some note and a plan to bring the milk and cheese industry into our living rooms, via our newly acquired TV sets. This was the kind of set that was most likely rented and would take a minute to warm the tubes before the grainy picture magically emerged from the large and very heavy screen.

MMB's advertising campaigns were ubiquitous; everywhere you went in the UK you would see poster campaigns, TV adverts, magazine and newspaper advertising:

> *– Milk, The Vitality Drink*
> *– Milk, Big Lift That Lasts*
> *– Milk, Nature's Nightcap*

CHEDDAR FOR THE MASSES

Coming from Somerset grasses
They are fashioned, I've heard
From heavenly curd
Aged in a clever mixture of moisture and air
With daily dedicated parental care
Months of turning and yearning
Bringing salt crystals and a burning
Desire to impress
The Somerset folk aren't known to mess
With recipes travelling through generations
Bringing savoury delight to many nations
Who are hooked on this cheese
In the fridge there to please
On the occasion you wish
For a toasty, bubbling savoury dish
But take care now to wait
Let it sit on the plate
For a while there at least
Because don't get me wrong
It will burn hell out of your tongue!

Sean Wilson, 2022

ACT III OF THE MODERN CHEDDAR:
UNIFICATION AND CHOICE

The industry was embracing the now post-war 20th century of opportunity, and from here the country was quite literally rebuilding. Housing estates were built to replace heavily bombed regions, but also in greenbelt areas, made free to use for the national building programme. Communities were constructed in clusters and would become instant places to live and work.

They were very much sought after by the 'new' families of the 1960s with 2.6 kids. Local schools and pharmacies were built to serve the needs of the community and people travelled into their market town for fruit and grocery, fish, meat and cheese. Life was free from war, the UK was benefitting from the availability of work and cars, and luxury items were available to families where both parents worked while the kids were at school – not the one breadwinner story of the past.

The emphasis was on fresh and wholesome and artisan, where families were able to choose their diet from what was readily available in their local markets.

Life was good again.

The situation was an improving one too, with the introduction of Mervyn Morris's electric milk float, sold to Roddington Dairy early in 1951. A resulting order from United Dairies saw the production of a three-wheeled, chain-driven vehicle, which was an immediate success.

Milk floats were designed to deliver milk silently and directly to the customer's doorstep and to be billed for at the end of the week. The silent delivery of gold top milk in the early hours was an ingenious concept and the whole country took to this new wave of milk delivery. Fast forward to 1967, where the UK Electric Vehicle Association announced in a press release that Britain had more battery-driven vehicles than the rest of the world combined.

Milk floats were a cheeky British hit. Benny Hill's Ernie was in his milk cart with horse Trigger, shooting out with his rival 2-ton Ted from Teddington in his bakers van. They were number one in the charts and Ted was proudly driving the 'fastest milk cart in the West'. A strawberry flavoured yoghurt won that day!

You may remember.

These floats were delivering more than just milk. There were now the ubiquitous Cheddar and eggs too. All was good in the world of milk and the country loved its 'Daily Pinta' from the MMB advertising campaign. We were drinking our way to healthy, strong bones and the war seemed a long time ago.

They were bringing milk to our door and serving our convenience.

Enter, the world of the supermarket. The one-stop shop to cover all your weekly needs for groceries and fruit, fish and meat; all under one roof and with a number of tills to help you pass through the checkout more quickly. The Co-op had a loyalty scheme, rewarding people with myriad 'gifts' for being loyal shoppers. The manifesto of the supermarket was to:

Have the buying power to buy in bulk and therefore to buy cheap. It was a service for you to utilise and was there for you. They formed a co-operative lifestyle, giving the shopper a home to buy their wares, to be able to compare products in the same genre and make decisions on what were their family favourites. Above all, it was convenient and cheap.

To be honest, it took time to entice the housewife away from shopping locally. She would still pour into town on a Saturday to shop at the family butchers in the market hall. Markets were traditional and each stall formed long-cherished relationships with shoppers that often spanned generations. You could buy cheap there too, but had the feeling of belonging to this era and being responsible for the livelihoods of the traders. It was a status quo that worked well, and does so even today.

The supermarket was good at pragmatism, at stacking shelves until they bulged with all the products you'd seen advertised on TV. But they were serving you as a unit and the profit of dinging tills was the paramount achievement at the end of a busy Saturday.

There was suddenly a world of choice and every genre of shop, from the local corner grocery store to the biggest and highest-shelved supermarkets, were all vying for our pound. We had choice in bucketloads.

But what was happening behind the scenes was the introduction of the American blueprint for sales. America had had supermarkets for years before the UK. Processing had redesigned the way of life over in the States; and it was cheap. In the UK a food could be processed for a cheap base price, but it would still be charged at an artisan price, as 'Something new in this line, madam.'

Profits were large and the advertising was backed by millions of pounds' worth of corporate belief. It was a mould already working in the States and would slowly but surely finds its way into the more watchful life of the British housewife. For instance, the milk shelf had a 'condensed milk' to choose now and plastic pots of yoghurt, buttermilk and soured cream. All were products made from processing; but what did we know about the science of processing in the swinging sixties? Nothing was known other than that the housewife had a lot to choose from; and that was good:

Evaporated milk: concentrated to one-half of its original bulk by evaporation under high pressures and temperatures, without the addition of sugars and usually contains a specific amount of milk fats and solids. It now has a shelf life of up to fifteen months.

Condensed milk: evaporated milk with sugars added, to be canned for consumer use or use in ice-cream processing and sweets manufacturing.

Pasteurised milk: the whole milk is brought, very quickly, up to 72°C and then cooled. This process just protects us from microbes that could be damaging to certain sections of society. It is simply pasteurised for health reasons only. It has a short shelf life and is useful as part of a balanced diet, giving us vital amounts of calcium and protein. The fats in milk are great for children as it provides essential vitamins for a healthy childhood.

From an epicurean point of view, there is only one choice with these milks, but this is the modern world of choice, variety is ever present in every department and the choice is yours.

This leads us to price wars and debates around quality, because supplying the world with decent Cheddar was now the challenge.

FINALE: THE PEOPLE'S CHOICE
LATE 20TH CENTURY AND THE CHEESE MARKET

The 1970s through to the turn of the century were smooth and business was keen but fair and the more traditional Cheddar was finding its way to market. There were new companies flooding the scene with 'marketable' Cheddar, and all was healthy in love and war, as they say.

The quandary of supply had now become acute and the machine of production and supply was the daily challenge – and distribution was a new factor adding extra spice to the mix.

Milk supply and EU workforce demands were challenges, but both were necessary obstacles to bring about growth in this sector, and 'growth' was a key word throughout this time. If a company could handle the expansion of volume and maturing at one end, to the price agreements with supermarket buyers and subsequent distribution at the other, then all was on track. It was a daily challenge, but was not insurmountable. This continued apace and, inevitably, quality standards became the difference on the shelves.

COMPETITIONS

These modern times have brought about industry standards awards ceremonies, where the industry gathers the world's finest cheeses under one massive, air-conditioned roof as big as two football pitches; where 250 judges compare 5000 otherwise anonymous cheeses, in hundreds of classes, in the search for excellence. This has an enormous boost for producers' reputations and is keenly fought throughout the frantic day of judging. Class winners become the best cheese in the world at that moment, adorned with silver trophies, rosettes and accolades galore. It is the perfect opportunity for the industry to open its doors to the public and hopefully impress them with the sheer size of the worldwide cheese fraternity.

The Cheddar category is one of the keenest-fought sections and as many as 150 whole cheeses in three different categories are competition-wrapped and dressed up – like a poodle at Crufts – a perfectly groomed block of uniform coloured Cheddar. Twenty kilograms of excellence is something to behold and it will be fashioned by each company's 'expert' dresser. There aren't many of these dressers to the pound nowadays, and they are jealously protected by the companies, as their talent can be the difference between winning and losing.

COMPETITION COMMERCIAL CHEDDAR CRITERIA

Firstly, overall appearance is important: wrapping quality and tightness with no loose or baggy areas of wrapping, it should be tight, but not to mis-shape the block; perfect 90° angles are a must, as appearance accounts for a lot of points, even before tasting! Colour and mottling are the second criteria: mottling can be a mark of a healthy cheese as the result of good maturing, an effect that pleases the eye. Too much contrast though will mark you down as it is a sign of an inferior cheese. Good natural colouring from the natural making and maturing process – no extra colouring should be needed at this level. The management of maturing gases can be important too, where discolouration and aroma can be affected.

But if all is well, we then enter the cheese with a cheese-iron; you may have seen one already, but the iron is T-shaped, the handle is horizontal and the iron is at 90° and is scooped and sharp. We push the iron into the cheese and we are looking for some resistance, but not too much. The resistance should have a smooth and creamy feel to it and need some effort to push through the cheese. We twist the iron and then pull out a 'plug' of Cheddar. This plug is then examined for creaminess, which will show on the back of the scoop with a uniform creamy slip of cheese from top to bottom of the iron. Too much creaminess will leave a skid pad on the iron and we will expect inferior qualities from here on in. We know now if we like the cheese or not – before continuing with our inspection.

We now study the aroma of the plug. We are looking for a depth that pleases both the nose and palate – a deep and multi-levelled aroma with nutty, hay tones, a deep savoury sweetness with distant notes of caramel (sometimes) and the far off, pleasant aroma of a farm. By this stage, if we are happy with the cheese, we are normally drooling and ready to taste it. A creamy and consistent light coating of the palate is a good first sign, before the deep, nutty, savoury sweet taste builds into a crescendo giving off, sometimes, a distant dry grassiness.

This should all be combined with a sharpness of finish that massages the tonsils and creates that uncontrollable, mouth-watering effect. It will be a great cheese, indeed, in my book, if it hits all of the above criteria, and will be marked high and earmarked as a contender at the end of the first round.

At this point it should be said that the quality of these commercial Cheddars will vary. But there will be definite similarities in flavour, due to the requirements of mass production, making any judgements difficult to detect. In this category, you have to show true mettle to define the good from the not so good.

We may have fifty to sixty Cheddars to taste and will have a supply of apples and water at hand to help the palate maintain some neutrality before moving on to the next entry. Having tasted all of the entries, we then gather the top four to five cheeses to re-taste them and decide the class winner.

This cheese is now the category winner and is recorded as such and then taken to the 'top table', a long series of tables where all the class winners are gathered for further inspection by our cheesy boffins, who will then choose the overall top three cheeses of the day.

The Cheddar categories in the competition are:

Farmhouse Mild Cheddar
Farmhouse Mature Cheddar
Farmhouse Vintage Cheddar
Traditional Farmhouse Cheddar

We have been studying the commercial classes of Cheddar, but you will see the addition of Farmhouse Cheddar; which is just what it says, a cheese made in the traditional manner, using animal rennet and sometimes unpasteurised milk, keeping as much as possible to the recipe devised by Joseph Harding back in the 1800s. They will be proudly displayed in 20kg, mostly cylinder-style, buttered-cloth binding to give a fully traditional appearance. It's a great line of historic Cheddars to be examined in the same way as the above.

In this class there will be marked differences in texture, aroma and flavour; which should be expected, since these cheeses will be indicative of their exact location, of herd, the grasses they fed on, the dairy practices and maturing. Each cheese typifies these criteria, displaying diversity as a direct result of all these natural elements.

Personally I love this category and baulk at the actual differences in the farmhouse cheese class and flavours, spanning a massive range. I guess, since it is made with unpasteurised milk and animal rennet, it will be just the same as the cheeses made hundreds of years ago. This is wholly the attraction to farmhouse Cheddar-making and carries a mark of pride for the producer.

Some farmhouse Cheddars hit the mark of excellence, but will be totally different to the commercial flavours – all down to these fluctuating environmental circumstances. Lovely creaminess is a standard requirement, but of course there are fluctuations even in that. I would say texture is the biggest difference and this will denote just how well the cheese was made at the outset. A cheese made on a cold and rainy day might be totally different from the same cheese made, at the same farm, with the same milk, but on a clear, warm summer's day.

It really is that finite, I believe, and although these cheeses will not be entirely what the supermarkets are looking for on their cheese aisles, they will be considered a marque of distinction on the 'specially selected' shelf. You will definitely find these cheeses in quality cheese emporiums, some delis and farm shops. You should seek these cheeses out too in your quest for great Cheddar. We will touch on this later.

There are a growing number of these international awards ceremonies throughout the calendar and you must try to catch up with one on your travels. They really are fascinating to experience – viewing and tasting the best cheeses the world has to offer. A cheesemeister's dream!

ANNATTO

So, throughout time, golden cheeses were richly hued in appearance, like the deeply coloured Double Gloucester. The county's longhorn cattle produced a lovely coloured milk, but this herd suffered a plague in 1745, and so the longhorns, that produced this beta-carotene-rich milk with a yellow hue, were wiped out in one fell swoop. The farmers and cheesemakers picked up the pieces and slowly they reintroduced a herd to continue making their sought-after, yellow-shaded cheese.

Markets were the sole sellers of local cheese and the Gloucester was popular; the colour was lovely and the best coloured cheeses would be snatched up first.

Following the cattle plague, cheesemaking continued, but the colour of the fresh herd's milk was much lighter and the cheese lost its rich colour; much to the annoyance of the locals. Something had to be done to remedy the situation and a whole host of colourants were used, but they either tainted the taste or were just not the right colour.

This was a period in history where great trade routes opened up and merchant ships were travelling the world to sell their wares, in the earliest efforts to export indigenous produce. Ships from Latin America sailed to our ports with goods and it was found they were carrying a seed from the achiote tree, which grew in sub-tropical regions at 1000m (3000ft) above sea level. It had a pink flower with a spiky, heart-shaped fruit capsule that contained about fifty bright-red annatto seeds. For thousands of years the Latin American Mayans had been drying and crushing these seeds to make face-paint for their religious ceremonies.

The Gloucester cheese community thought they would try this seed as a colourant in their efforts to find the right hue for their cheese. It was found that, with practice, a lovely yellow colour was possible. It was rich and pleasant to the eye and, furthermore, there was no tainting of flavour as the ground seed was tasteless. The right colour had been found and the cheeses of Gloucester returned to their favourable colour and all was good. The Red Leicester used the same method to create its red colour, and in time the Cheddar-makers were adding a small amount to their vat of milk to bring about a golden hue to their cheese.

The fact that annatto has been used for 300 years is an amazing success story for this little seed. The practice of using annatto to colour foods was taken to the absolute extreme. Yoghurts, butter, custard, puddings and, of course, cheese were all using the annatto seed to enhance colouring. Even ladies' lipsticks used annatto! Your Pink Pearl, New York Apple and Russian Red were all using our Latin American seed.

In the year 2000, the EU decided that the colouring in Cheddar was deemed to fall into the nut category and therefore its use banned from the production of any mass-produced Cheddar cheese. So, the rich, golden Cheddars we had become so used to were not rich and golden any more. You will notice the colour difference when you're next in the supermarket. The colour now is pale and somewhat insipid, as opposed to pre-millennial Cheddars.

I guess there will always be work afoot in the laboratories and in the logistics centres of the Cheddar trade to improve the status quo. As Cheddar had to relinquish its lovely golden hue and was left looking insipid, work was going ahead to see if any flavour improvements could be made to outshine the loss of colour. There was much debate in the labs to find some clue to help the situation. I think more by luck than pre-determined efforts, there were visits to Europe to investigate the nutty flavoured Comté and Emmenthal cheeses of the Alpine regions of the French/Swiss border; just to see if there could be some improvement made to the pale Cheddar.

Notes were taken, no doubt, and off to Italy they went to talk to the Parmesan producers of the northern regions. More notes were taken and they returned to the UK to unravel the notes. There was found to be a common denominator in the notes of all the cheeses. In their cultures, there was a different amount of a culture called lactobacillus helveticus. So, experiments went ahead to add tiny amounts to the cultures in the Cheddar cheese. I guess there were many attempts to define the correct mix, but it was found that the common denominator was working and it was improving nuttiness but also the savoury depth of the cheese. There was a marked improvement: the cheese was the same, yet different.

It was just like the flavour volume button had been turned up a little. Nowadays, most Cheddar in the cheese aisle will have this flavour improvement. You may have noticed in recent years that Cheddar has improved and I think it is for the all-round good of the cheese.

I have tried the experiment of pairing young Parmesan with mature Cheddar and there is a lovely similarity in flavour profile; not the same, of course (try it), but there is a similarity, nonetheless. All this work goes on to benefit our Cheddar. These companies are continually trying to bring us the best product at the best price – yet they are still able to keep to traditional values and balance this with a worldwide distribution network.

THE SILENT CHEESE-MAKER

Yes, there is a silent cheesemaker that exists in every cheese. Once the curds are cut, scorched, Cheddared, salted, pressed, and have left the dairy, the cheese is finished. The cheesemaker has used his or her experience to fashion the pre-determined quality of milk into the best representation of their artistic self.

This is what we believe happens to a vat of milk before we see the cheese on the shelf; packed and ready to peep its way through the checkout with you. We have touched on the maturing period with Cheddar, but only the lightest of touches.

The maturing period is arguably the most important and defining time for a cheese.

If a cheese is fashioned by an expert cheesemaker, but then matured by the directions of an amateur, the cheese will likely be sub-standard or spoilt for consumption – it is that crucial. The French call this vocation 'affinage' – the quest for patiently transforming the fashioned cheese into a 'great' cheese with care and daily attention. After all this devotion, the cheese will be 'affine a coeur' – ripe to the heart. Affinage takes a cheese from the bland and aroma-less curds into a flavourful, fragrant and beautifully textured cheese.

Cheddar takes three months to mature for mild, twelve months for mature, and eighteen months to two years for vintage.

Ripening cheese for longer periods of time develops the aromas and flavours in a great Cheddar. Affinage is the one craft that brings out the character of a great Cheddar. Each Cheddar is wrapped and then boxed; the box keeps the cheese square and thus saves on wastage at the packing point. It is then introduced to the maturing room. In the case of mass-produced cheese, this will be of warehouse size; and will be part of a series of high-tech warehouses.

Records will be taken of the day it entered and it will be placed in the hands of the maturing team who then choose the right temperature zone, according to the amount of time required to satisfy the strength criteria. The curds are moist at this point and one of the requirements of good affinage is to entice the moisture from those curds over time. The environment will have to be temperature-, humidity- and ventilation-managed to entice this moisture from the centre of the cheese.

It will be manhandled often, and washed, turned by the maturing team, keeping solely to the pre-destined rules, but using accumulated knowledge and intuition; using the above criteria to slowly draw out the moisture, which is already working on it and turning it to amino acid and tyrosine. As these acids build up they eventually crystallise.

SALT CRYSTAL CRUNCHY CHEDDAR

Through time the amino and tyrosine acids will be drawn from the centre and out of the cheese. As it very slowly travels out it will leave a 'crystal' deposit behind at random moments and in the case of the lactobacillus helveticus cheeses of Cheddar, Parmesan, Comté and alike, this crystal deposit helps to create a crunchiness to the bite of your chosen cheese. You will have noticed at the very least this same crunch in good, ripe Parmesan. It is a mark of a well-matured and affine-managed cheese. It is called 'calcium lactate', whereby in essence the cheese lactates the moisture from the inside out; thus 'lactating' – a term given to breastfeeding a baby, where the mother's milk comes forth from inside the breast.

UMAMI

'Does the crystal taste of salt?' is the question always asked by Cheddar-lovers about this crunch? Well the answer, rather disappointingly, is no. There is no taste attributed to the crystal, but it is thought to enhance the enjoyment of a fine Cheddar by creating the mysterious 'umami' moment – a moment that fills a fifth basic taste and which sits alongside sweet, bitter, sour and salt. It was discovered by Japanese scientists in the late 20th century and they called it 'umami', which translates to savoury/deliciousness. It was a whole new flavour dimension that opens our brain receptors to greatness in a millisecond. The brain is always working to instantly detect flavours for warnings or acceptance. Over time our brains have been trained to protect us in this way, which is why we instantly know if we like a fresh oyster or not – at first taste.

We can train our brains to accept an oyster, if we are determined – so the umami then returns to send you into raptures of delight when you taste a class-one oyster, fresh from the sea. Umami helps you to detect amino acids and protein in the cheese and since protein is vital to your health, this is accepted by the brain. This umami moment is a fascinating 'fifth' dimension and there are many meals created by Michelin chefs that embrace it, where a course is managed to bring just the right balance of flavour to send you into raptures of foodie delight.

This effect is found in certain foods naturally: meats, shellfish, fish, (including tinned fish), seaweeds, tomatoes, avocados, mushrooms, garlic, peas, cheese.

And most fermented foods carry natural umami: soy sauce, sauerkraut, miso, kimchi, yeast, green tea, Marmite, aged cheeses.

The brain loves these foods and is content to accept them as good for us, keeping us healthy with proteins and vitamins as an automatic reaction to the fifth-dimension flavour. It really is a fascinating subject on its own and would further delight from more research.

This is the effect of calcium lactate crystals in your fine aged Cheddar.

The management of these crystals is part of the maturing team's mandate, to create just the right amount – sometimes a big crunch, and sometimes just the lightest detection of a crunch.

SELF-AFFINAGE

So, once you have bought your great Cheddar, off the shelf or from the farm shop/cheese emporium, you will then become the affineur, and are then able to add to the affine of the cheese by good domestic management. You are now part of the maturing team, either keeping it in perfect condition or adding to the maturing period by just finishing the flavour for the best taste.

This domestic maturing is another vital aspect of cheese management and needs to be somewhere near correct or the cheese will just diminish – by drying out, or by losing taste, or by being kept too warm, or by being opened for a quick cheese on toast and then loosely re-wrapped in the same wrapper and put in the wrong part of the fridge. You may have spent good money on your great Cheddar; you may have used your knowledge from this book to help direct you to a great cheese. This same cheese needs some appreciation from here on in.

AFFINAGE AT HOME

First of all, you will need to decide what you want to do with the cheese. Some Cheddar is now dated for up to twelve months, best before – check carefully. If you pick up a twelve-month dated cheese, you could leave it in the wrapping and just let it mature further – until it is 'affine a coeur'. You could buy two of this cheese, eat one, and leave the other to mature. You may be looking to eat it with family and friends in a week or so before it 'goes off'.

If this is you, then you need to listen up.

To avoid a cheese 'going' before you need it, make sure you buy the cheese well – all best-before information will let you know most of what you need. Conversely, if you're in a cheese emporium, tell them what you are looking for and they will do the rest. If from a supermarket, take the cheese out of the wrapping and wrap it again in either tinfoil or greaseproof paper. Take an airtight container and a sheet of kitchen roll. Fold the kitchen roll lengthways into a 3-ply/3-cm-wide fold. Very lightly wet the kitchen roll under the tap – just a light touch of water will 'dampen' the roll. Lay it in the bottom of your airtight container, lay the re-wrapped cheese

in there, on top of the dampened roll, and close with a 'click' of assurance.

If leaving for a long time, you should leave it in the salad drawer of your fridge – which happens to be the coldest part of the fridge; or move it up the fridge as you approach the day of your party with friends. Keeping your cheese this way will dramatically lengthen its life, possibly by an extra month or so. So, in the end you will be buying great Cheddar and fully enjoying it for what it was meant to be. You will never need to throw away cheese ever again!

We need to think about our food wastage and we can all improve our fridge management. Essentially it will be saving you money too. Domestic affinage is a no-brainer for the cheese-lover. Find yourself an airtight cheese box – one for hard cheeses and one for soft. You will become quite the expert at affinage and this new skill will serve you well.

Try it with some of the softer Camemberts and Bries – a perfectly ripe Brie de Meaux is something to behold. Ask for a young Camembert with the intention of 'bringing it on' yourself. I urge you to try this and to spread the word with your circle of friends.

Saving money, saving waste, saving good cheese.

THE ENIGMA OF SMOKED CHEDDAR

THE ROYAL FLUSH OF CHEDDAR FLAVOUR

For me, cheesemeisters, any additive in Cheddar is most likely there to mask the inferior flavour profile from a poorly made cheese. This has long been a tactic to rebrand Cheddar, to make it marketable again, and we should be diligent when we choose an additive Cheddar. But, if there is a winner in this genre of additional flavour, it is the fabulous addition of smoke. The age-old art of cold-smoking a cheese and thus re-visiting the flavours of the deep past is very high on my all-time favourite flavours. Cheddar takes very well to an artisan smoke flavour. For me, there are very few cheese flavours to beat properly smoked Cheddar; evoking times where the fire was the main source of heat in a single dwelling, housing all the family; where the smoke permeated the dwelling and thus tainted everything, over time. I guess the Romans were involved in this activity, as they were the first to start aging cheeses in the pioneering stages of understanding and nurturing cheeses. There is a moment that causes me to pause and lightly touch, somewhere in my psyche, a head-space warmth of fireside camaraderie and flame watching; we all know this feeling and properly smoked Cheddar does this to me. The enigma I refer to in the title here is that the actual history of smoking cheese was never documented and therefore is lost in the distant time; and, because of this, creates a further stage of mystery that attracts my curiosity too. There aren't many foods that escaped the shackles of history, tying it to a timescale and thus pigeonholing it for the rest of time. Smoked cheese is one such product and I love it even more for this.

My personal favourite that takes me directly to this place is Montgomery's Smoked Cheddar – traditionally and carefully smoked to deliver the right flavours. There are other companies who smoke their Cheddars, but be aware that some of them are smoked with a 'liquid smoke' in the making process. These cheeses taste of heavy smoke and remind me more of kippers than cheese, so just be vigilant when choosing. Try searching for 'artisan smoked cheddar' and you will be sorting the wheat from the chaff. The other thing with smoked Cheddar is that a little goes a long way, as it is rich, so be frugal when adding it to a recipe and use a 'smoked cheese' box to store the cheese.

If, like me, you love a good smoked flavour in your cheese and you are yet to try smoked Cheddar, put it on your bucket list of flavours; you will not be disappointed. Deal yourself a royal flush and go all in on this one, cheesemeisters.

A smoked Cheddar has the ticket to ride
Through the fields of bountiful taste
As rich as the squire sat there princely inside
That's where the knowledgeable embrace
The secrets of alchemy passed
And Smoked Cheddar will have amassed
A following of smoke and of dagger
That secretly line the fortunate cracker

A TALE OF TWO AMBITIONS

Just as is the case with my Lancashire cheeses, the main effect on the character of a cheese is the *terroir*, the area where the X-factor of geographic features align in such a way that the area becomes special for cheesemaking. This geographic alignment of features is very prevalent with Cheddar cheese too. It could be argued that the theatre of unique cheesemaking alignment is at its best in Somerset. From the Bristol Channel there are several river systems wending their path through the Cheddar-making county of Somerset. A prime example of great cheesemaking topography with regards to Cheddar is the River Brue valley, where the slow-flowing, small-to medium-sized English river allows essential water to be man-managed through a series of sluices and floodgates and distributed wisely to create a double benefit. The main benefit is the management of the flood plain of the Somerset Levels, which eradicates potential problems of flooding around the Glastonbury region. Cheese has been made here for over a thousand years, and this is where the gentle topography offers rolling pastures and all this needs water to feed it. The second benefit being the human element, which is important here too, I think. This manifests itself with the joining of hands of the cheesemaking fraternity. There is a Somerset *joie de vivre* that lends itself to a friendly cheese-farming infrastructure; most cheese farmers are happy to join forces and help each other out when needed, and this partisanship could be the key to a good amount of the Cheddar-making success story.

The Brue Valley Living Landscape is an ecological conservation project based on the Somerset Levels and Moors and is managed by the Somerset Wildlife Trust. Subsequently, this conservation initiative belies the importance the valley has for the English landscape league of importance. All the above reasons are essential for supplying the aforementioned X-factor of farming essentials to aid the making of excellent Cheddar.

The Brue, geographically, is twenty miles south of the Cheddar Gorge, and here I thought we should look at the topographical differences of the two Somerset areas to fill in the *actual* story of Cheddar cheese history. In my opinion the best Cheddar cheese was, and still is, made through the more southern Brue Valley, utilising the carotene-rich rolling sweep of lush pastures. This is where the Cheddar was made. The cheese was then transported by horse and cart to the Mendip Hills area, a rugged twenty-mile trip north of the valley, to a series of rocky limestone gorges called the Cheddar Gorge. The caves within the gorge were used to house the cheese in the Mendips town of Cheddar. The cheese was then ripened in the 12°C atmosphere of the caves before it was released, as and when needed, to the negotiants and consumers. The cheese was *made* in the Brue Valley and *ripened* in Cheddar, yet the town name of Cheddar was the name given to the cheese. I think the utilising of the rolling pastures and the twinning with the limestone caves was key to the success of Cheddar in the Middle Ages, as the ripening of this cheese is essential to its rich qualities and therefore the stratospheric rise of popularity through those times. Nowadays, the cheese is still made in the X-factor-rich valley of the River Brue, but now it can be ripened in the purpose-built modern warehouses, on or near to the Brue Valley cheesemaking farms. Cheddar, on the whole, does not rely on the caves any more.

So, I'm visiting two cheesemakers in the more traditional Somerset-cadenced towns of North Cadbury and Bruton, both in the heart of Cheddar-making country. They are split only in their Cheddar-making ambition. Cheddar through the ages has been divided into two camps and this is why I wanted to interview one of each in this category.

Both camps are *Farmhouse*, although the farmhouse category is split into *Traditional Farmhouse* and *Farmhouse*. The *Traditional Farmhouse* producers are making their wares with completely historic methods and ethics; unpasteurised milk, on the whole (some use pasteurised) but using age-old

methods and with tradition at heart. They produce less volume, but the flavours are considered to be more historic and truer to the original recipe of Joseph Harding. The *Farmhouse* method is to make cheese with pasteurised milk and old starters, thus producing *cleaner* cheese with a depth of rich, creamy qualities for the more global needs in this genre. This allows the output to be much larger and helps feed the demands of the global market.

In the tiny and very English village of North Cadbury, sat in the heart of Englishness with some thatched and all stone-built houses, I have to slow the car down. The mood here is Dickensian and we actually feel a reverence to a time past. White washing flaps on the washing lines and the stone has the chalkiness of age, the chiffchaff warblers' refrain is loud, and we are searching for the home of Montgomery Cheddar; age-old Cheddar-making at its best and in the totally traditional style. We are in the heartlands of Cheddar-making country, as we are not far from the River Brue. You can actually feel the slower pace of life here. We could easily be in Dordogne.

We have to visit the village store to ask for directions to the farm; the very same village store that survives mainly on sales of Montgomery Cheddar; and the main outlet for this fine English cheese. I am guided down the country road to be met in the farmyard by James Montgomery, with straw in his hair! After pleasantries, it's a dash into the house for James, leaving the question, 'Tea? Coffee?' just lingering in the air as he sweeps inside. On I follow excitedly, armed with questions and a camera.

A very friendly and, dare I say, a pleasing, slightly bohemian farmer with the definite *joie de vivre* of a true Somersetonian; and with the passion that is Montgomery, James tells us they are third-generation cheesemakers and how it all stems back to Grandma and her 'house cow'; where each farm would have a cow to provide milk, at the very least. Cheesemaking started on the farm in 1911, and is totally unpasteurised, uses animal rennet, and a starter from Barber's Cheddar. This starter has seen years of development and carries the heartbeat of Cheddar-making at its core. The starter is a culture of friendly microbes that are essentially *fed* on a daily basis and are used often in this style of cheesemaking. They carry the self-generated *gene* through husbandry, these microbes are cared for with as much care and attention as any of the cattle; they are the midi-chlorians of cheesemaking and can be over 100 years old. So, safe to say, the ingredients in James's cheesemaking carry integrity. James's rhetoric then relaxes, and we talk about the Brue Valley X-factor of 'just the right location' and the 'luck' he has had being brought up just here in North Cadbury. 'All the stars come into line here for cheesemaking and with a little guidance we fashion totally traditional Cheddar of some quality,' he proudly explains.

I ask if he feels the cheese is made in the field or the dairy. He thinks it's a good question and after some thought says, 'I think it's a balance of the two; cheesemaking is about balance from start to finish and the fields are just as important as the fashioning of that milk. We are a good community of cheese farmers, we look after each other and this harmony brings a balance too.' A good point, well made, I think; and they are lucky to have this harmony.

In tasting Montgomery, I find a total antithesis between *Traditional Farmhouse* and *Farmhouse* Cheddar flavours. His cheeses are rich and earthy, with a tone of farmyard about them, which I love in French cheeses also, and we talk about how that Cheddar flavour quality will develop over as long as five minutes, and it does! A taste of times past, and a multistage marque of distinction, is how I would describe it in broader terms. There will be more variation in flavour from batch to batch, but this is to be applauded within the fraternity, it seems. The smoked version is phenomenal.

'We have 200 Friesian cows and some Jerseys. We produce about 100 tonnes a year, serving some UK retail and exporting quite a bit to the USA.' James feels that the British supermarkets can be fickle in their treatment of great Cheddar products and does *some* supermarket business.

He also sells his cheese at the aforementioned local village store. As owners of the store, Bob and Jackie New sell his cheese either there in the store for daily, local, and wider community needs, or online. James says that his cheese is probably responsible for the village store's survival and is happy to help the shop along with this philanthropic deal. A breath of fresh air indeed in these times of profit and loss, deadlines, and logistics.

This is the total charm of Cheddar folk. The *joie de vivre* I referred to earlier is infectious and this friendliness carries to the other cheesemakers in the valley too. This is good, old-school husbandry, and I am bowled over with this Somerset *economy of need* for the 21st century. 'If they want it, they'll come, and if they don't, they won't,' is where James sits here.

Indeed, they mostly do come, cheesemeisters like me. Just order online and the deliveries go out every Tuesday; I totally love it!

We never got that tea or coffee!

There are just five makers left in the UK of clothbound *Traditional Farmhouse* Cheddar and I have listed them for you here:

Montgomery Cheddar: **village.stores@yahoo.com** for online sales

Keens Cheddar: **www.keenscheddar.co.uk** for online sales

Quicke's Cheddar: **www.quickes.co.uk** for online sales

Westcombe Cheddar: **www.westcombedairy.com** for online sales

Hafod Cheddar: **www.thecourtyarddairy.co.uk** for online sales

There are other outlets for these cheeses, just check online.

And so, on to Bruton, the town on the Brue, where my friends at Wyke Farms Cheddar reside. The Clothier family are owners of 1500 acres of surrounding land in the protected valley, which is key to a lot of their success. This particular area is alive with Cheddar history. As far as the eye can see there are gentle slopes aside the main throat of the valley, following the course of the river and just downstream from the lovely Glastonbury Levels.

The family have farmed here for generations. The climate is gentle and mild, bringing warm air from the sea in the summer, mist and rain through the winter, providing the best conditions in the world for dairy farming. There is main road access, but it is hardly a *main road* as I know it, and farm traffic must struggle from time to time with oncoming traffic as they approach. This farm has adapted from its meagre beginnings and their footprint has grown accordingly, but it still has the same cottage *Farmhouse* kerbside appeal.

We take the back roads and imagine ourselves in France. The design of the farm properties here definitely favours beauty over functionality. There are 'Wyke' signs attached to most of the farms we pass, for one reason or another. The whole area is predominantly of Wyke domain as they employ a large proportion of their staff locally. They are a much larger concern than James at Montgomery and I guess it would need to be if they are to supply to 165 countries worldwide with *Farmhouse Cheddar!*

On site we are welcomed with the same *joie de vivre* already mentioned. A tight hug of friendliness from all belies the genuine company ethics here of hard work backed by cool people. In fact, the company mantra passed down by Grandma to John, the elder Clothier, is:

Good, Better, Best
Never Let It Rest
Until Your Good Is Better
Than Your Best

A good solid message for any hard-working company, methinks. The Clothier family have been making cheese here for 160 years, when their revered Grandma Ivy was making her Cheddar and Grandpa Tom knew that Cheddar-making was an art. Wyke's ethics are generally quite simple: To make a *Farmhouse* cheese with their secret family recipe (from Ivy) in a completely sustainable circle of production. To spread the Wyke ethical map far and wide around the world, thus educating the world with great Cheddar flavour excellence.

As mentioned earlier, the *Farmhouse* cheese is made with pasteurised milk and first on the list of sustainable reward is the awarding of a *bonus* better price to any supplying farmer who can show sustainable profile in his yield. This is then backed up with age-old cultures passed down from Grandma. This is the simple formula creating a rich and multistage flavour of a climbing vintage flavour, culminating in a good calcium-lactate-crystal *crunch*. A *Farmhouse* flavour of some distinction in my book, this cheese has won more awards for flavour than any other Cheddar, and rightly so.

The technical director, Diane Cox, oversees this flavour profile with her inimitable focus on detail and she doesn't take any prisoners when it comes to Wyke's *Farmhouse* flavour. Each batch carries her stamp of approval, and her special skill is to grade a ten-day-old curd and predict its projected profile quality in eighteen months' time. Quite some skill! All of Wyke's focus is on flavour, and it shows.

The bigger Wyke commitment to the Brue Valley is interesting too, as moving forward they are committed to the environmental landscape. Through the initiative of their owner, Rich Clothier since 2012, Wyke are now the most sustainable company in Europe. They are backed up by their 2014-commissioned 500kw bio-gas installation, powered by farmyard manure and waste dairy products, as well as local farmers' 'misfit' vegetables. The installation is then twinned with their impressive solar energy site and the combined green energy provides all production and office needs, as well as tractors and farm traffic, while feeding the surplus back to the grid. Environmental best practice of feed management, soil and grass regenerative farming programmes are in place too. Wyke are leaders in dairy farming sustainability technology and the blueprint of Rich Clothier's making demonstrates the family's vision of the future that can be utilised globally to help create a net zero carbon baseline for future herds and dairy farming worldwide.

Cheddar is helping the future of dairy farming for the greater good and this commitment, twinned with the Somerset *joie de vivre*, is a potent mix that just deserves continued success.

That said, the mainstay of British sales is ironically with Aldi and Lidl, who love all of the facets above, and are committed to their company's sustainability, making for a strong future of mutual respect. Other smaller supermarkets stock Wyke cheese, but the big four are busying themselves with own-brand Cheddars and their associated profits. So Wyke have concentrated their efforts on the more 'sustainability friendly' European and global markets, who understand and reward renewable energy companies with shelf space. They now sell to 165 countries worldwide.

As far as I'm concerned, and for what it's worth, this model of farming and superb cheesemaking is in a good place, employing flavour with a net zero carbon position and is setting Wyke up for an exciting future in the capable hands of Rich Clothier. Wyke are making good clean sense and are ploughing furrows of legacy that should and will carry Cheddar into the future.

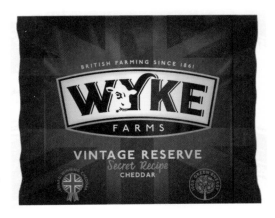

This is how Wyke Farms present their cheese – much more professional and 21st century

THE CHEESEMEISTER'S GUIDE TO THE 'NEW' CHEESE EMPORIUM

The *great* need for British cheese in these post-Brexit times is to keep educating the cheese-loving public. We need a place where we can hear the real stories of all our territorial and new cheeses and this is high on my agenda; a place where cheese stories can be told with a passion that matches the efforts put in on a daily basis by our British cheesemakers.

The rural machine of the early morning milking of cattle and the subsequent channelling of the milk into the vat, to then let the cheesemaking team fashion cheese, is their daily chore. We have an ever-present, fast-moving world to live in and we miss the real stories going on out there.

I have brought you the story of Cheddar which has unfolded well here and the cheeses have been well, *and rightly*, represented. The great shame though is that the book needed to be written in the first place. There is very little education out there on our indigenous cheeses and this book has attempted to put the Cheddar story in the public consciousness. The passion of Cheddar-making is alive and kicking in the UK. There are Cheddar-makers in Somerset, Dorset, Wiltshire, Cornwall, Scotland, Scottish Highlands, Isle of Man, Shetland and Ireland. Some of these Cheddars are supplying supermarket 'own brand' shelves and this is the train of supply and demand, all very quickly and easily stacked high on the shelves; a convenience for the modern, busy consumer.

There is though a growing family of British Cheddar cheesemakers turning out fabulous cheese with farmhouse quality. Each of these brands needs the right representation on the shelves, so that their efforts are *fully* appreciated and thus become a supply chain to appreciative Cheddar-lovers. The British cheese-lover needs an outlet of supply that is friendly and informative and can source the great cheeses this country has to offer. The big brands are looking after their own concerns very well, and with sales teams of quality they are selling their wares far and wide around the world. But where do the rest of us have to purvey our cheeses? We gather awards and plaudits, but the world of commerce chases the big brand, leaving other *well deserving* companies behind.

Enter the world of the *new* cheese emporium. A growing number of shops are popping up around the UK, where the owners have taken the massive career jump and entered the world of cheese. They have loved real cheese all their lives, but have now taken the leap of faith to become commercially involved. I think these emporiums are immense and I applaud all of them for making their great decision to open for business. The new cheese emporium has ambition and this ambition is *real*, to match the passion that originally attracted them in the first place. The world of social media is ubiquitous and can be utilised quickly to become a platform to extol the virtues of their wares. As soon as you enter their shops, the passion is tangible and this enthusiasm is there for all to see. They are involved in mail order, so delivering great cheese to your door. There are great 'Cheese Nights' cropping up, where customers can get involved in some grading of cheese, with a glass of wine and a score sheet; learning about cheese in a friendly environment.

What more can the cheese-lover want? A knowledgeable service, delivering really impressive cheese at an affordable price, somewhere near where you live. And if it's not where you live you can buy online from this good and worthy supplier, thus helping a dedicated service. These guys are holding the future of cheese education right there in their hands. The old, and sometimes quite snooty, cheese shop is quite rightly becoming outdated and should put their efforts into their customers in a friendlier and real fashion, I think. Times are difficult right now for the newbie cheese emporium owner with rising post-Brexit prices and all the other negatives of logistics and packaging price rises, but it's the *raw passion* of these emporiums that the convenience cheese world didn't account for. THIS IS THE FUTURE OF BRITISH CHEESE. I feel that strongly about it.

We are a nation of cheese-lovers (unless we have dietary differences that don't allow cheese or take a stance against cheese). We all have a piece of Cheddar sat there in our fridge and now from this book we are armed with lots of recipes to utilise your cooking needs, with fun and imaginative ways of using and keeping good Cheddar. We do though need to find a reliable supply of great Cheddar. If this book has done anything it should give you the impetus to want to spend your hard-earned cheese money in the right place. Use the internet to your advantage and find these new businesses, they are out there, and help them move along in the right direction, backed by your interest and dedication to their passion – a mutual passion in cheese. This is the only way forward for British cheese and the sooner we mobilise and show our strength as consumers the better. The cheese-lover wants to find pride again in our cheeses, free from European rules. This *is* the time for us to realise our power as consumers and to patronise and support those who we recognise as having our best interests at heart; who respect and appreciate us.

Post-Brexit times should be great times for British cheese to flourish.

If you hear about a great cheese or find one at a country fair, you should be able to ask your local emporium to look into adding it to their range. They will be happy

1: with your enthusiasm

2: you are helping them improve their stock

This is the new way to shop for cheese, I think. The world of consumer awareness is here and we will shop according to the new rules of engagement; passion being the number one requirement!

I have taken the initiative to demonstrate one such business in Crosby, Liverpool, who have done exactly what I have described above. They have given up their previous jobs and gone *all in* with a new business, supplying their customers with all the above. The business has fulfilled its first year and owners Lee and Debbie Zeverona are showing a trainload of dedication; and lo and behold it is paying off in ways they never imagined. The interest shown in their business has been immense and this is *exactly* what I've been alluding to. We love our cheese and we just need to be able to find it in a friendly, informed way. Just look at their counter bursting with great cheese at affordable prices, all served by informed members of staff, who bust a gut to help you out. PASSION right there, cheesemeisters! You'll see they have special nights on a weekly basis, providing a community hub of cheese-lovers who can then move on together. EDUCATED about great cheese.

Crosby Cheese and Charcuterie: www.crosbycheese.com

The Cheese Shop, Morpeth: www.thecheeseshopmorpeth.co.uk

The Calder Cheesehouse: www.caldercheesehouse.co.uk

The Cheesebox: www.thecheesebox.co.uk

Love Cheese, York: www.lovecheese.co.uk

George and Joseph Cheesemongers, Leeds: www.georgeandjoseph.co.uk

Just use one of these dedicated shops for the delivery of your preferred cheeses, or Google businesses closer to home to assist your needs.

These businesses need our support and are powered by knowledge and customer craft to bring you fine cheeses stacked with history, all of which couldn't be easier to access with the internet.

If you make today the day you change your Cheddar ways it will repay you in dividends.

BREAKFASTS

CHEDDAR AND PANCETTA OMELETTE

SERVES 1–2

Where the egg meets wonderfully savoury Cheddar and pleasingly crispy and slightly salty pancetta. A simple yet crazily tasty breakfast. There is a knack to the omelette and we will focus on the controlled simplicity as we go. Suffice to say, sometimes it's the simplest of ingredients that please the palate most. The focus here is the quality of the ingredients, as there are only four: fresh, free-range eggs, fine vintage Cheddar, crazily thin Italian pancetta, and a knob of butter. A reliably non-stick frying pan and the handle end of a wooden spoon paired with a great plate and freshly ground black pepper are essential.

EQUIPMENT:
24cm non-stick frying pan
Wooden spoon
Kitchen roll
Measuring jug
Pepper grinder
Great plate
Small plate with kitchen roll

INGREDIENTS:
5 slices thin pancetta
Knob of butter
4 medium, fresh, free-range eggs
15g vintage Cheddar – grated
Salt and pepper

METHOD:

In a measuring jug or something similar, break the four eggs and set aside.

Warm the dry frying pan for 2 minutes and neatly lay the pancetta in the pan, side by side. Turn up the heat until they happily sizzle. Have an implement handy for turning them over. After only a minute, turn them all over and wait for them to crispen. Have the small plate ready with kitchen roll to drain the pancetta, which will now cool and crispen up.

Turn down the heat and leave for a minute or so before very briefly whipping up the eggs with a fork. It is important here to just whip for 5 seconds – you just want to break the yolks really.

Pour the eggs in the pan and turn up the heat slightly – just a touch. With the handle of the wooden spoon, carefully bring in the egg to the middle of the pan. Start at 12 o'clock and bring to the middle, then ten past, quarter past, and so on. There will be a nice mound of egg in the middle but the raw egg will cook on the outside.

On one side of the omelette, sprinkle over the Cheddar and break up the crispy pancetta. Season with a little salt and a good grinding of pepper.

Now you need to use a little intuition here, insofar as you don't want to overcook the omelette. So with some runny egg still visible – but not lots – take your spatula and slide it under one side of the omelette. This side will now be (boldly) folded on top of the underside, forming a half circle – a simple and bold fold, nothing more or

less. Don't worry if it's slightly off-centre – you can remedy that on the plate. Cook for a minute.

Now, go over to your plate and slide the omelette onto it. Take the kitchen roll now, lay on top and this is the time to re-shape slighty, as well as absorb some of the fat from the top. Season with a grind or two of pepper.

You should now have an omelette of some distinction – a nicely shaped half circle, ever so slightly runny in the centre, seasoned to perfection, and ready for the breakfast you deserve.

Of course, this omelette recipe is there for you any time of the day, but breakfast is best!

CHEESE ON TOAST – MODERN (V)

SERVES 2

The humble cheese on toast; the working-class meal of heavenly cheese on crispy yet giving toast. Cheap and simple are the two criteria here for the classic. Here we are modernising the classic, but with cheap ingredients that totally jazz up the party, making it shine like a culinary star. We match the sharpness of the Cheddar with the creamy, stringiness of grated mozzarella. We then add the modern, savoury, jammy quality of an onion sauce. This addition of sweet and sharp – yin and yang – red onion balsamic sauce, underneath the pillow of Cheddar and mozzarella mix, gives the springboard needed to launch this recipe into the umami stratosphere. I use a good thick slice of sourdough bread, which when toasted lifts it into the ranks of 'heavenly'. The Cheddar will repay careful selection manyfold, so be careful when looking for the right cheese.

EQUIPMENT: Frying pan, 2 mixing bowls

INGREDIENTS:

2 thick slices of sourdough bread

100g sharp Cheddar – grated

80g mozzarella – grated

120ml crème fraiche

1 egg yolk

Seasoning

Good ketchup

Red Onion Sauce:

Dash of olive oil

1 medium red onion – just chopped, chunky

½ red pepper – medium-sized, chopped

2 cloves of garlic – sliced

Pinch of chilli flakes

3 sprigs of thyme – leaves separated

1 level tbsp sugar

3 tbsp balsamic vinegar

METHOD:

In a frying pan, add the dash of olive oil and when up to heat add the onion, garlic and red pepper. Cook out for 2 minutes before adding the sugar and chilli flakes. Spin them around to amalgamate. Add the balsamic vinegar and allow to mingle, boil and reduce to a jammy consistency. Set aside.

Turn the grill on to high and set the grill tray down one notch.

In a bowl, throw in the cheeses and mix, add the egg yolk and crème fraiche. Mix thoroughly and season well. Set aside.

Toast your bread until nicely browned and crispy – don't butter.

Spoon half the red onion mix onto the toast and top with a good handful of the cheese mix, so it sits nice and high on top of the toast. Sit this onto a baking sheet, ready for the grill. Repeat with the remaining toast and then carefully slide under the hot grill. Keep an eye on this now as the grilling will take hold of the cheese and will melt/brown it at different rates with different grills. You are waiting for the top to brown in a way you will rarely have seen from cheese on toast, with the melting of the cheeses underneath. You will know when it's right. Carefully take from under the grill and slide them onto a cutting board, hot and steaming. Scatter the fresh thyme onto each piece of toast. Slice and allow to cool for a minute before diving in!

Enjoy with good ketchup and heaps of freshly ground pepper.

Nom!

WELSH RAREBIT (V)

SERVES 4

Saturday morning is the time to contemplate this Welsh rarebit: cheesy, beery, spicy heaven on a plate. Just one pan needed for this one, leaving you time to pick out the form in the 1.10 at Kempton, maybe. If ever there were a man's cheese on toast, then this it! N.B. While you're checking the quality of the field, check the quality of the Cheddar, because if I were a betting man, its quality will come through in the end, just like a great jockey.

EQUIPMENT:
Medium, heavy-bottomed saucepan
Wooden spoon
Grater
Small bowl
Baking tray
Racing Post! And a pen ...

INGREDIENTS:
30g butter
2 heaped breakfast spoons of plain flour
1 level tsp of mustard powder
Good pinch of chilli flakes
200g vintage Cheddar
5 tbsp London porter beer – or Guinness
4 slices of great sourdough bread

METHOD:

In the bowl, mix the dry ingredients: flour, mustard, chilli.

Turn on the grill and take the grill down one level from the element.

In the saucepan, throw in the butter and melt. Chuck in the flour mixture and mix thoroughly with a wooden spoon to combine well. It will be thick and crumbly. Cook it out for a minute, to cook out the flour taste. Add the beer and start mixing it into a smoother mix for 1 minute. Add the grated Cheddar in two batches and melt into the mixture. You should have a brown and smooth mixture – don't overwork it or the cheese will let go of the oils. Mix for 2 minutes at most on a medium-low heat. If too thick, add some more beer, but not much.

Set aside.

Cut 4 thick slices of sourdough bread and whack under the grill to brown one side. Take out of the grill and with a breakfast/dessert spoon filled with rarebit, turn the spoon over and, using the edge of the uncooked side of bread as your lever, empty the spoon onto the toast. Repeat this with about 4 other spoonfuls, so it sits nice and high above the bread. Smooth it off with the back of the spoon. Repeat with the other 3 toasts.

Whack under the grill to brown the rarebits to your desire.

Season with freshly ground pepper and maybe some ketchup – it's up to you.

Enjoy!

FRIED CHEESE AND HAM SANDWICH

SERVES 2

If you are a lover of the cheese toasty for brunch or supper, or a weekend get-together with friends and a few beers, these cheese and ham sandwiches are for you. They tip the scale at 'excellent' and you should make them knowing you're going to impress with these little beauties. I use a joint of ham which I just thinly slice from for this sandwich, keeping the rest of the ham for another meal. This ham has the best flavour and can be sliced to your preference. It is a simple recipe with great ingredients.

EQUIPMENT:

Mixing bowl

Grater

Scales – maybe

24cm non-stick frying pan

Pastry brush

Olive oil

INGREDIENTS:

250g vintage Cheddar

1 heaped tsp powdered mustard

1 tbsp Worcester sauce

Pinch of chilli flakes

Freshly ground pepper

2 egg yolks

Slices of ham – to suit your appetite

4 slices of thin white bread

Olive oil for brushing the bread

A dash of beer – if needed

METHOD:

In your mixing bowl, grate the Cheddar and add all the other filling ingredients. Mix thoroughly – if too thick add a dash of beer to help you out. Add the egg yolks before the beer, if needed.

Take the bread and paint the bread on one side with olive oil. Turn one over and place the sliced ham on there. Push on half of the cheese mix and push it down firmly. Lay the other slice of bread on top – oiled side up – press down the whole sandwich with your palm. Repeat with the second sandwich.

Heat up the frying pan and add a tsp of olive oil. Lay one sandwich on the pan at a time – cover with a pan lid if possible to circulate the heat – and cook for 4 minutes per side, or until they are nice and golden.

Serve with the warning that it will be hot! Or wait a few minutes before devouring.

49

49

COWBOY RANCH BAKED BEANS

There once was a cowboy from the prairie
Who needed beans but (really) dare he?
Sat making a fire on a moonlit night
His lighter flickered as he put the fire to light
'Cause out here folks the beans ain't tinned
The forecast was clear but with gathering wind.

SERVES 4

Shop-bought baked beans are stacked with fibre and proteins, all good and amenable, but they have at least 5% sugar and are part of the over-sugared processing problem we are all having to manage in the face of global obesity. I don't get involved with tinned baked beans for this reason, so I have always made my own. These beans are the epitome of home comforts. Smoky and cheesy and fresh, cooked from scratch with ease and no frills, just cowboy beans given their finest hour. Kept in the fridge, these beans are an obvious rollover for further dishes.

INGREDIENTS:
A splash of groundnut oil or dripping
100g smoked bacon lardons
1 onion – chopped
3 cloves of garlic – chopped
Fresh rosemary and thyme – tied together
400g tin cannellini beans
400g tin tomatoes
Good squirt of tomato puree – sun-dried is best
Up to 1 tbsp balsamic vinegar – to your taste
1 level tsp sugar or 1 level tsp tamarind
Sprinkling of smoked paprika – to your taste
Sprinkling of chilli flakes – to your taste

METHOD:
Take a medium/large pan and throw in the groundnut oil or dripping. Heat until smoking hot. Add the smoked lardons and cook until crispy and smoking. Take out the lardons with a slotted spoon and reserve – the lardons will render and leave some of their lovely natural fats in the pan. Add the onion, garlic and cook through. Add the beans and tomatoes, then give a swirl before adding the puree. Just check the consistency of the beans here – if too thick just simply half fill one of the empty tins with water and pour onto the beans. Add the tied herbs and cinnamon. Bring to the simmer, then add the smoked lardons, smoked paprika and chilli flakes – give another good swirl. Add the balsamic vinegar, and sugar or tamarind, and stir in.

Put the lid on and very gently simmer for up to half an hour.

With 5 minutes to go, remove the herbs and cinnamon, and then throw in the Cheddar/mozzarella mix and really incorporate.

The cheese will have brought a saltiness, so you may only have to season well with freshly ground black pepper.

When serving, you can throw over some more grated Cheddar if you wish.

The obvious accompaniment would be a baked potato, but crispy, scratch oven chips would be great too.

Or:

Good quality butchers sausages would be the best double up.

There you go, pardner!

SUNDAY MORNING CHEDDARED SCRAMBLED EGGS (V)

What can be finer than a sneak into a Sunday morning kitchen to rustle up some scrambled eggs for your significant other? Just the two of you enjoying some of the delights that eggs can bring us. This is the simplest of recipes in this book but they still need some finesse. A plate of these creamy eggs, well seasoned, letting the Cheddar wink at you, is just as amazing as the most complicated meal. For instance, the famous king of chefs and chef of kings, Escoffier, says that his scrambled eggs were 'scrambled with a fork, with a clove of garlic on the tines.' But I think a simpler approach is a good starting point here: quality fresh eggs, good butter, great Cheddar, and salt and pepper, will suffice here, methinks. No amount of milk or cream will make properly cooked scramblers any better. Butter and eggs only in my scrambled eggs – just cooked lightly and not scrambled beyond belief, with a slow action, lifting the lightly cooked egg from the bottom of the pan. Trust me – take care and they will repay.

METHOD:

2 eggs per person is enough to satisfy a Sunday hunger, cracked and emptied into a clean bowl. Inspect for bits of shell and discard.

Lightly beat the eggs, just pulling the yellow and white through each other – no more.

Heat the butter in the non-stick pan and pour over the eggs and work them lightly with a wooden spatula – gently laying the cooked egg on top of the uncooked.

Add as much cheese as you think sufficient so as not to prolong the cooking period – about 10g per person, as a guide.

You're not looking for fluffy qualities – once they lose their liquidity, I take them off the light heat to just then coax the eggs together.

Season with good salt and grinds of pepper.

Serve immediately, remembering the egg will carry on cooking.

Maybe on sourdough toast – liberally buttered with real butter.

Simple, but perfect.

A LOVERS' CHEDDAR FRITTATA (V)

SERVES 2

The origins of the frittata are Italian and I guess this is set in stone, but the Spanish have their version, officially known as tortilla. The tortilla/frittata is classically cooked with potato and egg though; but when did peasant dishes ever have an official title? Never. I have based this frittata loosely on a Spanish theme, combining the Spanish sunshine ingredients of red pepper and peas with fresh thyme and rosemary and mushroom. The common adjoinder here, of course, is a good Cheddar, either vintage or (my preference here) farmhouse vintage, giving the earthy qualities of unpasteurised milk and bringing a savoury creaminess, just gently joining the ensemble to bring a bit of sunshine to this breakfast/brunch dish. A sharer through and through, the frittata is the food of love and should be enjoyed with your significant other, over a small glass of Pouilly-Fumé or white Rioja. The frittata has a knack for bringing you over the plate, so as not to drop any egg – thus bringing the loving couple together.

Un Amor Compartido!

EQUIPMENT:

24cm non-stick frying pan
Vibrant plate
Grater
Bowl to mix the eggs
Hand whisk

INGREDIENTS:

Shallot – peeled and chopped
¼ of a red pepper – finely chopped
3 sprigs of thyme – leaves separated
1 sprig rosemary – leaves separated and chopped fine
4 Chestnut mushrooms – chopped
Fresh or frozen peas – a handful
Knob of butter
1 tbsp of olive oil
6 eggs
30g good Cheddar
Pinch of smoked paprika
Salt and pepper

METHOD:

Heat the oil and butter in the frying pan, add the fresh thyme and rosemary, and leave to just sizzle lightly – imparting their flavour gently to the oil. Now turn up the heat and add the shallot, red pepper and mushroom, and sizzle for 4–5 minutes, but don't colour them too much.

In the meantime prepare the eggs. In a bowl, crack the eggs and grate the Cheddar over the top. Season with a little salt and lots of pepper. Whisk to combine all the ingredients.

Pour the eggs over the ensemble in the frying pan and turn down the heat to low. Add the peas now – you just want to cajole the eggs into setting – nice and slowly. We are looking for a good colour on the bottom of the pan, as this will eventually be the top and we don't want to burn it. Cover the pan with a lid. Anything will do, but

it needs covering.

The cooking of the frittata is all about the gathering smell in the house as it cooks. When you hear a few bubbly sizzles, after say 8–10 minutes, you are ready for the fun to begin.

With the plate in your hand, place it over the frying pan to cover the whole pan. Carefully turn everything over to allow the frittata to drop onto the plate. Lift the pan to reveal the good colour you have achieved. Slide the frittata back into the pan and cook the bottom of the frittata for 4 minutes to finish the job properly.

Repeat the turning over procedure again with your (cleaned) plate and you will need to season with salt, pepper and a pinch of smoked paprika. You now have a lovely frittata to share with your beloved.

Enjoy.

EGGS EN COCOTTE (V)

Now here is a dish of lovely simplicity, perfect for a Sunday morning for you and your partner; just chilling. All you need is a couple of ramekins and a loaf tin; a pan with mushrooms and courgette, cooked in butter, an egg and Cheddar with a swirl of cream. Really it is a lusciously soft and yellow yolk, baked in a water bath to perfection, and with the addition of some fresh dipping bread, it's a luxurious, simple treat. Known in France as oeufs en cocotte and devoured in Parisian cafes on a daily basis, we can make-believe we're in Paris while we consume this eggy and Cheddar luxury.

EQUIPMENT:

1 small pan
2 ramekins
Grater
2lb loaf tin
Tea towel

INGREDIENTS:

Butter to grease
2 medium eggs
Knob of butter
3-4 chestnut mushrooms – chopped
½ courgette – sliced and chunky chopped
Salt and black pepper
Cheddar cheese

METHOD:

Pre-heat oven to 180°C.

In the small pan add the butter and fry off the mushrooms until they give up their juices. Add the courgette and cook with lid on for a minute. Season and leave aside.

Fill and boil kettle.

On your work surface have your two buttered ramekins ready for use. Spoon in the mushroom/courgette mixture. Grate over with Cheddar. Crack an egg and carefully let it drop into one of the ramekins, on top of the mushroom/courgette mix. You have an option here to grate over some more lovely Cheddar. Place into the loaf tin and put onto the oven wire rack, ready for pouring the boiled water into the tin. Pour to halfway up the outside of the ramekin and carefully slide into the pre-heated oven (10 minutes for soft egg or 12 minutes for harder egg) and the Cheddar beautifully melted on top.

Use the tea towel to carefully lift the ramekins onto two plates – season with freshly ground black pepper and serve immediately.

This is a lovely alternative for a Sunday morning breakfast or supper.

STREET FOOD

MUMBAI STREET FOOD STACKER

Street food is the hot choice these days. Where the imagination of the privateer can come forward, giving the streets a myriad options, variety being the key to an Indian street's food choices. The vibrancy of central Mumbai is alive with Asian primary colours and the mixing of smoky food smells of fish, meat and BBQ, making for a more festival atmosphere than a city centre. This is a bona fide way of meeting friends and catching up, over a stacker of shami kebab, stacked with oozing coriander yoghurt dip and hot sauce. Dill pickle, cucumbers and tomatoes are the perfect addition to your stacker under the makeshift Mumbai canopies. I have compiled a recipe for the authentic shami kebab here. This underrated kebab is burger-shaped and stacked with spicy Indian flavours. The drive of using a shami is the really soft and giving texture of the patty, adding to the essential good mouth-feel-comfort required for a testing stacker. Once you're committed to this high-rise burger you will need to keep a grip on it from thereon in! The perfect prerequisite for any good street food. Hold on tight!

EQUIPMENT:

Large, wide, heavy-based pan.
2–3 mixing bowls

Hand blitzer or liquidiser
Plate for cooling
Set of tongs

INGREDIENTS:

Shami Kebab:

100g chana or toor dhal – soaked in water for an hour
220g minced lamb
2 medium onions – chopped
6 cloves of garlic – chopped
400ml water
½ tsp salt
Nam pla or lime juice – optional seasoning, instead of salt
1 inch piece of ginger – peeled and finely chopped
1 green chilli
2 tbsp groundnut oil or mustard oil
Pinch of chilli flakes – to suit your tastes
Handful of fresh coriander – roughly chopped
1 tsp of garam masala or Sri Lankan garam masala
1 tsp cumin seeds
1 egg – beaten
2 tbsp plain flour
1 bottle sunflower oil

Shami Filling:

1 red onion – finely chopped
1 green chilli
Juice of 1 lime
Palmful of mint leaves
Pinch of sugar
Pinch of salt

Stacker:

Tomatoes
Large dill pickle – sliced
Red onion
½ cucumber – sliced
Hot chilli sauce
4 tbsp plain flour

Yoghurt Sauce:

400ml yoghurt
80ml milk
Handful of fresh mint – or 1 tsp mint sauce

To Finish:

30g each of Cheddar – grated
Chilli flakes
Lime juice
Suitable burger buns

METHOD:

Firstly, we want to start the kebab in the traditional style, by whizzing up the onion, garlic, ginger and green chilli in a liquidiser, or a hand blitzer, until smooth and creamy. Take your wide and large pan and heat the chosen oil to then throw in the onion mixture and cook on a light simmer for 10 minutes.

Add all the lamb mince and the drained chana dhal. Just about cover the meat with about 400ml water. Bring up to the boil and then simmer for 20 minutes. Add the salt and uncover the pot for 10 minutes or so – until the meat mix starts 'catching' on the bottom of the pan – showing the evaporation of liquid is working. All excess moisture has to evaporate.

Transfer to a plate and set aside to cool – 15 minutes.

Transfer the cooled mixture into a liquidiser or use a hand blitzer to blend to a smooth paste. Add the coriander and chilli flakes, garam masala, cumin seeds, and season with salt – or fish sauce (nam pla) and lime juice – and blitz until smooth again.

Tip this mixture into a mixing bowl and add the egg to bind everything together. Now add the flour and mix thoroughly.

In a separate bowl, mix all the shami filling ingredients and set aside.

Shaping the Kebabs:

Wet your hands and take a handful of shami mixture. Flatten the mixture on your hand and push an indentation in the middle. Spoon in a teaspoon of filling mixture and then work the kebab mix 'around' the filling – totally enveloping the filling mix. Shape into a patty – a round burger-style shape, 1cm thick. Set aside.

Repeat the process, allowing two kebabs per person.

Yoghurt Dip:

In a bowl, mix the yoghurt with the milk and add the fresh coriander and fresh mint. Whizz up with a hand blitzer and then add salt and chilli flakes to suit your taste. Set aside.

Constructing the Stacker:

Split your burger bun into two halves. Spoon yoghurt dip onto each half. Then squirt on your chilli sauce. Stack up now with tomato and red onion and then set aside.

Now for the cooking of the shami. In a bowl of flour, dip the kebab in there and lightly cover with flour. Bring your oil up to heat in the frying pan and then fry the kebabs on a medium heat – turn the kebabs with your tongs – until coloured well on either side. If they colour quickly, turn down the heat a little. Beware of undercooking the kebab – you could store them in a warmed oven if you want to.

Take the cooked kebab – two per person – and stack onto the tomato. Squeeze over the lime juice. Stack on the dill pickle slice and cucumber slices – sprinkle over the grated Cheddar and chilli flakes, and then crown with the top of the burger bun.

You might need to push a knife through the stacker from top to bottom to stabilise the construction.

This is a fab example of spicy street food. Commit and enjoy!

INDONESIAN CHILLI CRAB AND CHEDDAR PANCAKE (V)

SERVES 4

Indonesian food has a fascination for me because it covers myriad different styles of food. Spicy? Yes, definitely. Fresh? Absolutely. Innovative? Yep, to a massive degree. The fusion of various regional culinary traditions that form the archipelago nation of Indonesia has created one of the world's most exciting cuisines. I wanted to capture this fusion food in a grown-up style, giving a definite Eastern spicy freshness, whilst using the vehicle of a freshly cooked pancake – effectively a fresh spring roll without the deep-frying element. Quick, easy and burstingly fresh street food, with an eye on the balance of flavours. The Eastern 'fresh' approach has the added element of being high in superfood qualities and is therefore easily digestible because of the freshness. All of the above have attracted me to Indonesian cuisine throughout my cooking life, so I thought we would create this very achievable and fresh chilli crab pancake. I have added a creamy, savoury Cheddar here, but if you were in Indonesia you would probably be offered dangke, produced in the South Sulawesi region. Dangke is processed by boiling fresh buffalo milk with sliced papaya leaves, soaked in brine overnight before being wrapped in banana leaves, to mask the bitter taste from using unripe papaya. I think Cheddar will be a great substitute for dangke!

EQUIPMENT:

24cm non-stick frying pan

3 mixing bowls

Hand whisk

Grater

Kitchen roll

INGREDIENTS:

1 dressed crab – a good sized one

Nam pla – Thai fish sauce

Chilli flakes

Thai basil

Coriander – finely chopped

Large dash of white wine vinegar

½ cucumber

4-inch piece of mooli

8 thin slices of fennel

100g good sharp Cheddar – grated

Fresh lime juice

Sweet chilli sauce – extra fresh chilli is optional

Salt and pepper

PANCAKES:

150g plain flour

1 egg

Milk

Knob of butter per pancake

Chilli flakes

Salt

METHOD

Pickled Vegetables:

Firstly we should prepare the vegetables: the fennel, cucumber and mooli. Cut them all into julienne – sticks about 2–3mm thick. Place them in a bowl and add a good splash of the wine vinegar, and then pour over some boiled and cooled water to then cover the veg. Set aside in the fridge.

Next, prepare the pancake mixture. Combine the flour and egg and pour over just enough milk to combine them, by whisking. Add and whisk the milk slowly now until you have a single-cream consistency. Add chilli flakes to suit your needs and a little salt. Set aside in the fridge for at least half an hour.

Crab:

Spoon the crab from the dressed shell into a bowl and start to move it around with a spoon to bring out the creamy quality. Add a squeeze of lime juice and a splash of fish sauce. Have your chilli flakes to hand to season as required. Add some finely chopped coriander and mix through to combine. Taste, then set aside in the fridge.

Construction:

Firstly put your frying pan on a high heat – dry. When you think the pan is hot enough add a knob of butter. Whizz your chilled pancake mix with a spoon and pour enough for one pancake onto the fizzing butter. You want a nice thin pancake here, so a pour and swirl motion will help spread the pancake mix, rather than keep pouring to achieve a circle – a little mix, big swirl to fill the base of the hot pan will pay dividends. Cook for a minute and then flip to cook the other side. Set aside on kitchen roll. Repeat four times.

Collect your components on the worktop and you're ready to build your pancakes: crab, pickled veg, coriander, Thai basil, Cheddar, sweet chilli sauce and fresh chilli – all ready to go.

We will be stacking the pancakes on the nearest edge of the pancake to you, leaving a gap of 3cm either side to aid folding the pancake once filled. First crab, then veg sticks, then Cheddar, then chilli sauce or fresh chilli, then lime juice, and then finally the fresh coriander and Thai basil. Season with pepper only.

Push down all the ingredients with one hand, keeping it secure and start rolling the pancake – all the rolling will be away from you. Take the near edge of the pancake and start rolling until you meet pancake on the other side. Bring in the edges to form two ends of your pancake parcel. Continue rolling until you have a tight pillow of filled pancake with two blocked ends, thus completely wrapping all the ingredients. Lay the parcel on top of the final edge, thus using gravity to keep closed.

And Breathe!

Repeat four times.

Enjoy this ultra fresh and wholesome lunch.

NAPOLI PARADISO PIZZA (V)

The classic, original margarita pizza, born in Naples; loud and cosmopolitan Naples, the epicentre of big cosmopolitan Italian-ness, with a dark and dangerous edge. Where bread meets cheese; the Don Corleone of peasant food. A friend only to the right kind of food-loving epicure, the one who can appreciate the craft of bread-making to the next level. The patient chore of waiting for the dough to slowly create air bubbles as varied and light as clouds. Pure orbs of pizza joy that will provide a protective crust of crunch whilst harbouring a soft and giving artisan centre. The melding of the right tomato sauce and manfully ripped chunks of fresh buffalo mozzarella topped with slices of ripe tomato and a multi-layered, aged and creamy and slightly charred Cheddar. What is not to like?

All this is available to the home cook. Great pizza is not just for the realm of the uber hot Italian bread ovens, this same pizza is achievable from the domestic kitchen with this recipe.

Don't believe the hype, cheesemeisters!

Pizza is not just for speed dial.

Yes, it's probably as cool as it gets to drop into Napoli's finest and proudest pizzeria, but there is a domestic method of hitting that crazy, crunchy, artisanal height, and here it is: puro paradiso!

EQUIPMENT:

The bigger the baking tray, the bigger the pizza

Small pan with heavy base

Bread mixing bowl

Bowl to weigh

Scales

Bread scraper – find on Google

Oven gloves

INGREDIENTS:

Dough:

180g warm water (from tap)

4g dried active yeast

250g plain flour

Pinch of sugar

5g salt

Filling:

2–3 cloves of garlic – sliced

Fresh thyme leaves – stripped from stalk

1 tin of good pulped tomatoes

2 ripe tomatoes – sliced, but not too thinly

25g mozzarella – grated

A buffalo mozzarella

35g aged and quality Cheddar

Freshly ground pepper

Olive oil

METHOD:

This whole process will take around 3 hours.

Firstly, we need to prepare the pizza dough. Let's start with warming the bread mixing bowl in the oven – just give the oven a nudge around to 180°C for 3 minutes with the bowl inside. Turn off the oven and remove the bowl. Close the oven, trapping in the heat.

Add the weighed warm water (from tap) and add the yeast and a pinch of sugar. Leave to fizz for 5 minutes.

Weigh out the flour and salt separately, ready to add to the water when fizzing slightly.

Mix the flour thoroughly to create a shaggy mess – nothing very artisan comes from this first mix, so don't worry. Cover with cling wrap and slide into the warmed oven for half an hour. This is called autolysis. After the half hour, uncover the dough and add the salt, mix it through by hand (with wet hands) and start 'working' the dough with circular lifting motions – slightly lifting and caressing the dough to feel the softness. Now start the 'lift and fold', by lifting/stretching the dough at 12 o'clock, upwards to feel the 'stretch' and then fold in down, by pushing into the edge at 6 o'clock. Turn the bowl 90° and lift and fold again. Do this seven times, cover again and leave in the warmed oven for another half hour. Repeat this system of half-hour waiting – lifting and folding, four times in total.

You might need to give the oven a 'blip' of heat at some stage, if you feel it is cooling too quickly.

Leave this dough in the warm oven now for up to 1 hour. It will be rising in this time and is called the first rise and will double in size and create a bubbly surface.

In the meantime, prepare the sauce by heating the olive oil in the pan and adding the sliced garlic. On a medium heat, cook the garlic until golden and aromatic. Turn down the heat and add the thyme leaves to cook slowly for 2 minutes. Add the tinned tomato and thoroughly mix the ingredients together. Cook for 5 minutes on low and set aside.

Take the bowl of doubled dough from the warm oven and thoroughly flour your work surface or a large breadboard. Tip the dough onto the floured surface carefully. Flour the surface of the dough too. Take a bread scraper and slide it underneath the dough to lift one side, straight over the other, thus making a dough 'pasty' shape. Flour this 'pasty' well and cover with cling wrap to further rise – the second rise. This is the rise that will give you all your air bubbles, so try to keep it warm and let it rise naturally for up to 40 minutes. If the bread board fits in the warm oven, this would be a good environment for the dough.

You are now ready to make your pizza. Have your ingredients to hand and flour your large baking sheet or pizza tray ready for the dough. Take the dough from the oven and carefully peel back the cling wrap to reveal the warm and risen dough. You will need a bit of skill here to use the bread scraper to get underneath the dough and then quickly and carefully transport the dough to the baking tray.

Set the oven to its highest setting.

You can now start to shape the 'basin' to take the pizza filling. With the back of your hand start pressing down the centre, leaving an edge, and thus creating a pizza shape. A wall of dough will appear and can be encouraged by fashioning with your fingers and turning the tray – shape and turn – until you are happy with the shape. Less handling here is best, so don't overwork the dough.

First the sauce. Take a spoonful of the garlicky tomato sauce and lay 3 spoonfuls on the pizza base. With the back of the spoon, spread around to cover your basin. Add the grated mozzarella and sliced tomato. Top with ripped buffalo mozzarella and then the grated Cheddar. Season and slide into the middle of the hot oven.

It will take 10 minutes or so to cook the pizza. Try to 'vent' the oven by quickly opening the oven door from time to time to allow the moisture to escape – but keep your face away from the 'whoosh' of hot moisture.

After 10 minutes or so, when the dough has risen and is catching great colour, and the topping is melted and slightly charred, you should be ready to consider taking the pizza out of the oven. Be careful here, as everything will be uber hot and dangerous to touch – use good oven gloves.

You should now have a pizza of some distinction, ready to take on any 'artisan' pizza from Naples. Tap the crust and hear the quality. Let the pizza cool somewhat before considering a bite – it will be lava hot!

Goditi ogni boccone!

Enjoy every bite!

NEW YORK KNISH (V)

STREET FOOD FROM NEW YORK STATE
MAKES 7–8 KNISH

I can't fail to be impressed by the ingenuity of street food and for me this knish (pronounced kuh-nish) fits the criteria of creative street food. Firstly, I think street food needs to have origins from either harder times or from the traditional working classes, or both. Add to this some 100 or so years' history (at least) and you have street food right there – the history being the arrival of the Ashkenazi Jews of Central and Eastern Europe in the 1600s through 1900s into New Amsterdam, USA. Faced with economic hardship, and social and political changes, they fled to the then Dutch colony – which later became New York City. This migration grew more popular and in 1920 there were 1.6 million in the New York Jewish community. I think it's fair to say that the Jewish faith just loves their traditional recipes and knish was a beloved favourite of the persecuted classes. It was no surprise when these snacks became unilaterally available. Served warm, these hand-sized snacks are sold in either New York butchers' shops, bona fide knish bakeries, or on street-side, hot dog-style stands. I find this recipe nice to make and easy if you have 45 minutes to spare. The pastry just falls into place with these measurements, the filling takes just 20 minutes and you'll be styling out some real New York street food.

EQUIPMENT: 2 mixing bowls, 1 roasting tray

INGREDIENTS:

Filling
330g skin-on potatoes – quartered
1 onion – halved and sliced
1 tbsp sunflower oil
3 tbsp breadcrumbs – shop-bought are good here
3 pinches sugar
1 egg beaten – a little kept aside for glazing
100g sharp Cheddar cheese – cut into 1–2cm chunks

Dough
190g plain flour
1 tsp baking powder
1½ tbsp sunflower oil
1 medium egg
45g water
A little salt to taste
Freshly ground black pepper

METHOD

Have the 2 bowls to hand.

In a smallish pan boil up the potatoes for 20 minutes or until ready.

In another smallish pan fry up the onion on a high heat at first to give good colour and then medium to finish off.

While these are cooking out you can throw together the dough.

By adding all the ingredients into the bowl and mixing by hand until silky and smooth for about 2–3 minutes – no real kneading required, just combine well. Add more water if dry or flour if wet to balance the dough out. It should be very near to perfect though. Cover with a dampened towel, ready for the filling.

In the other bowl, throw in all the filling ingredients, and using the back of a fork squash it all down into a 'filling' consistency – not chunky, not smooth. Season up with salt and pepper and you're ready to go!

Have the oven on at 180°C.

Now you need to have some flour at hand to roll out your dough.

Flour the work surface and start rolling into a 12x9in rectangle, with the longest edge nearest to you.

Once happy with the size, take large spoonfuls of the filling and place them along the nearest edge, leaving a 2cm margin for joining the pastry. Egg-glaze the edge.

Now take the furthest edge and carefully bring it over the top of the filling (towards you) and join it to the egg-glazed edge you have prepared, essentially making a sausage shape.

Block up the ends by reshaping the pastry accordingly and then roll in the lightly floured work surface into the sausage shape.

Lightly mark your pastry sausage into 7–8 equal parts and then make a cut to start fashioning your first knish on the first of your marks.

Choose one end to be the bottom and shape a little to close the end and let it sit in your palm, bottom down.

Now gently push in the 'top' pastry towards the centre, but not all the way, to create a circle of viewable filling. Repeat right around the top and keep it symmetrical.

Once at this point you can now pinch the outside edges with your fingers while rotating the knish to make about five pinches, so you now have a bottom, a top with some viewable filling, and pinched sides. Place in a roasting tray lined with greaseproof paper – repeat until you have 7–8 knish.

Paint the rest of the reserved egg wash on the top of your batch of knish and throw in the middle of your oven for 40 minutes to bake them to a turn.

Smell the homely, cheesy baking aromas around the house as they cook.

Hanoe!

(Hebrew for enjoy!)

SCRATCH MEXICAN BURRITOS

SERVES 6

Food for me is all about that first bite, that first realisation as your taste buds give all the right messages that you've made something a bit special – that umami moment that we crave, when you look at your partner and realise you've cracked it. This tortilla is one of those dishes. The history of the tortilla goes back to the Mayans, 12,000 years ago, so in a way we are creating something with culinary alchemy – smoky and fiery black beans with perfectly seared beef steak and a sharp, citrus salsa. All cooled with a spoonful of soured cream and grated, sharp and creamy Cheddar cheese. A Friday night classic in my book, with a weissbier and friends … perfect.

EQUIPMENT:
24cm non-stick frying pan
2 mixing bowls
Grater
Medium saucepan

TORTILLA:

250g plain flour

½ tsp salt

2 tbsp olive oil

Combine the flour and salt in a bowl, then add the oil. Pour 150ml warmed water. Mix thoroughly into a dough and then knead on the worktop for 2 minutes, until nice and smooth and pliable. Cover and let it rest for 15 minutes. Cut the doughball into 6 and cover the other 5 as you take the first one in hand. On a floured surface, roll out as thin as possible – they should be about 20cm wide and 2mm thick. Heat the frying pan over a medium heat and cook each tortilla for a minute or so and then turn over, to make both sides golden and scrummy.

BLACK BEANS:

450 tin black beans – shop-bought

1 tbsp olive oil

½ onion – finely chopped

1 clove of garlic – chopped

Ground cumin – to taste

Smoked paprika

Salt

Chilli flakes – to suit you

METHOD:

In a medium saucepan, throw in the olive oil and then the onion and garlic until coloured. Add the beans and mix through, throw in the cumin, paprika and salt (to taste). Let the beans cook down dryish and mashable, and then mash with a fork. Set aside.

SALSA:

1 onion

1 green pepper

2 tsp capers

1 small carrot

Salt – to taste

Chilli flakes – to taste

Fresh coriander – finely chopped and to taste

Lime juice – to taste

METHOD:

Finely dice all the veg and add to a bowl. Season with salt and chilli flakes. Add the capers and fresh coriander. Mix through and taste. Then add the lime juice. Mix and set aside. Season with chilli flakes.

STEAK:

2 x 2cm-thick rump steaks – from the butcher where possible

1 tbsp groundnut oil

2 cloves of garlic

Good salt and pepper

To Finish:

40g vintage Cheddar – or to your taste

Dessertspoon of soured cream on each burrito

METHOD:

Make sure the steaks have been out of the fridge for over an hour – doused in oil and peppered, but no salt yet.

Take the frying pan and heat to hot. Add the oil and 2 crushed garlic cloves – skin on and just crushed – just before the steaks go in and salt them liberally.

Throw on the steak and hear it sear! Turn on the cooker hood too, you'll need it! Colour that side well before turning over to colour the other side the same. Turn down the heat and continue to cook for 3–4 minutes.

In the meantime, prepare your burritos:

First the still-warm tortilla:

Spread over the black beans, then spoon on the salsa, six times.

Take out the cooked steak and slice up good and thick.

Throw them on the salsa. Grate over the vintage Cheddar and top with a spoon of sour cream.

Roll and commit!

You have a ready-made party or a great Friday night in with your partner in crime.

VINTAGE CHEDDAR ARANCINI (V)

Here we have an authentic Sicilian arancini, said to be first recorded in the 10th century at the time when the island was under Arab rule. They were originated for the feast of Santa Lucia on 13th December when bread and pasta are not eaten. Today, arancini are a popular Western snack, found in delis across Europe and the States. A crunchy exterior guards a soft and creamy risotto interior, holding the jewel of melted vintage Cheddar within. This snack is best cooked as a definite rollover from risotto eaten the day before.

EQUIPMENT:
Medium/large heavy-bottomed pan – for deep frying
Mixing bowl, pan for stock

INGREDIENTS:
Leftover risotto of any flavour from yesterday
Or
1 tbsp olive oil
Few sprigs fresh thyme
½ onion – finely diced
1 celery stick – finely diced
2 cloves garlic – finely diced
200g arborio rice
Glug of vermouth
2 pints of good stock – or miso paste stock
100g chestnut mushrooms – chopped chunky
10g dried mushroom – steeped in a cupful of hot water for 15 mins – then chopped
Fresh tarragon
Single cream or plain yoghurt
Seasoning – salt, pepper, balsamic vinegar
3 tbsp Parmesan – grated

For the Arancini:
100g vintage Cheddar in 1cm chunks
3 tbsp plain flour in a breakfast bowl
Breakfast bowl of breadcrumbs – either stale and liquidised, or shop-bought breadcrumbs, or shop-bought panko breadcrumbs
2 eggs – in a breakfast bowl, whipped with a fork
Medium pan with 1 ltr sunflower oil
Kitchen roll – to drain

METHOD:

If using yesterday's risotto, just skip this section and go to 'Arancini Method'.

On a back hob, heat the stock in a pan to boiling, then simmer. Have a ladle ready in the pan.

In your medium/large deep heavy-bottomed pan, or equivalent, such as a Le Creuset cast-iron casserole pan, pour in the olive oil and allow to slowly heat. Throw in the sprigs of thyme and let them flavour on a low heat in the oil for 5 minutes. Discard the thyme now and turn up the heat. Add the onion, celery and garlic and lightly cook until translucent. Add the rice and incorporate with a wooden spoon to coat all the rice. Add the glug of vermouth and again swirl to incorporate. Add the stock – one ladleful at a time. Allow the rice to absorb the stock by continually swirling with a wooden spoon, until you feel it needs another ladle. Add ladlefuls this way for 10 minutes. Add the (chopped) reconstituted dried mushrooms. Swirl. Add the flavoured water from the mushrooms and really start to work the liquid into the rice by swirling continually – just a circular swirling motion, nothing vigorous. Add the chopped chesnut mushrooms. Add the chopped tarragon and swirl to mix. After 20 minutes of swirling, you are ready to start tasting and judging on seasoning. A tsp of balsamic vinegar here is good – swirl and allow to disperse. Then salt and pepper to taste. Add 3 tbsp of cream or 2 tbsp of natural yoghurt and mix. At 25 minutes your risotto is cooked. Add finely grated Parmesan to create a further creaminess, by swirling.

You need to let this risotto completely cool before making arancini.

This risotto will keep in the fridge for 3 days. If reheating as risotto, it should be fully heated through until piping hot, to eliminate bacteria.

ARANCINI METHOD:

Heat your oil in the pan – 3 inches deep is adequate for oil depth in the pan. Heat until a small piece of bread sizzles – then it is ready.

In the meantime, you can prepare the cold arancini. With wet hands take a palmful of risotto and shape into a ball. Push your thumb into the ball to create a cradle in the middle for a cube of vintage Cheddar. Roll again into a 2–3cm diameter ball, trying to keep the cheese in the centre. Prepare as many of these as you need and set aside.

Have your bowls of flour, egg and seasoned breadcrumbs ready.

Once the bread sizzles in the oil, turn down the heat to keep it at a safe temperature. Roll a risotto ball in the flour first, then the egg and finally the breadcrumbs. Then place the arancini on a spoon to carefully add to the hot oil – it should sizzle, but not a mad sizzle. Keep your eye on the heat of the oil. If the sizzle is not enough then turn up the heat on this first arancini.

An Arancini is done after 3–4 minutes and a lovely deep golden colour. Carefully take out of the oil and into a bowl lined with kitchen roll. Continue until all the arancini are done.

NEW YORK PORK AND CHEESE BUNS

MAKES 15

Known in China as gua bao, these pork buns are a product of the old and revered cuisine of Fujian. Originally steamed with stewed chai sui pork filling, the massive Chinese community of New York have used their westernised freedom of choice to create myriad recipes. All the recipes fill the main criteria of timing, able to be made through the morning, ready for lunchtime. These buns are served hot with the Chinese sweet and savoury soft chai sui filling and are a sought-after snack or lunchtime delicacy, found all over Chinatown. Here is my version using more readily available ingredients and creamy, sharp Cheddar cheese. We are using the recipe for the mainly Jewish challah bread dough. So, essentially this is an eclectic mix of the two very popular and important communities of New York in one snack.

EQUIPMENT:

Bowl for marinade

A lightly oiled bowl

Measuring jug

Bread bowl or KitchenAid fitted
   with dough hook

2 roasting trays

Scales

Greaseproof paper

Pastry brush for glaze

INGREDIENTS:

Marinade:

85ml dark soy sauce

2 tbsp brown sugar

2 tsp Worcestershire sauce

1 tsp Dijon mustard

3 cloves of garlic – chopped

2 tsp honey

1 tsp sesame seeds

Pork:

1kg of pork steak slices from the
   supermarket – these are great
   and cheap – cut into 1-inch slices

100g sharp Cheddar cheese –
   cubed into 1cm cubes

Challah Bread:

(Dry ingredients)

560g plain flour

10g dried active yeast

55g castor sugar

(Wet Ingredients)

180–200ml hand-warm tap water

2 medium eggs, plus 2 egg yolks

2 tbsp olive oil

Glaze:

1 egg in a cup – whipped with a fork

Sesame seeds

METHOD

Day Before Cooking:

Gather all the marinade ingredients in a bowl and throw in the chunky sliced pork. Cover and keep in the fridge overnight.

Cooking Day:

Take the pork and marinade from the fridge and set aside.

In your KitchenAid bowl or bread bowl, gather the dry ingredients from the bread list, and also gather the wet ingredients in another bowl. Thoroughly mix the dry ingredients before slowly introducing the wet ingredients whilst mixing at the same time. If using a bread bowl, just throw in the wet ingredients and work them in by hand thoroughly into a dough.

You may need more warm water to bring the dough together (I did) or you may need a little more flour if it's too wet. All that is good and this is the right time to do that.

Work this dough now for 10 minutes by machine or 12–15 minutes by hand, just until silky smooth and no need for a floured work surface.

Leave in the lightly oiled bowl and cover with cling wrap or similar and keep in a warm environment for 1 hour or more until doubled in volume.

Put the oven on to 180°C.

In the meantime, take the marinaded pork and throw it into the roasting tray, keeping the marinade to one side. Cook the pork for 30 minutes until just done and still a bit bouncy – not over firm. Set aside.

Take the doubled dough from the bowl. Pull off and weigh out 75g of dough. This will be your first pork and cheese bun.

In your left hand, flatten the dough by spinning clockwise and pinching with your right hand, thus flattening into a dough disc. Fill your dough disc with a mixture of pork and cheese – about 3 pieces of cheese and 4 pieces of pork.

We now need to envelop the filling with the dough. This is achieved through a pinching movement with your right hand. Start pinching the dough upwards to begin forming a ball of dough. Keep pinching and the dough will come together in the middle. Have a roasting tray lined with greaseproof paper and floured. Lay your first bun on there.

Repeat now until either the pork runs out or the dough.

Cover each tray with cling wrap loosely and allow to second rise – 1 hour or more.

Once risen nicely, glaze with the egg and sprinkle on sesame seeds. You are now ready to cook the buns for up to 25 minutes until golden brown.

Serve hot.

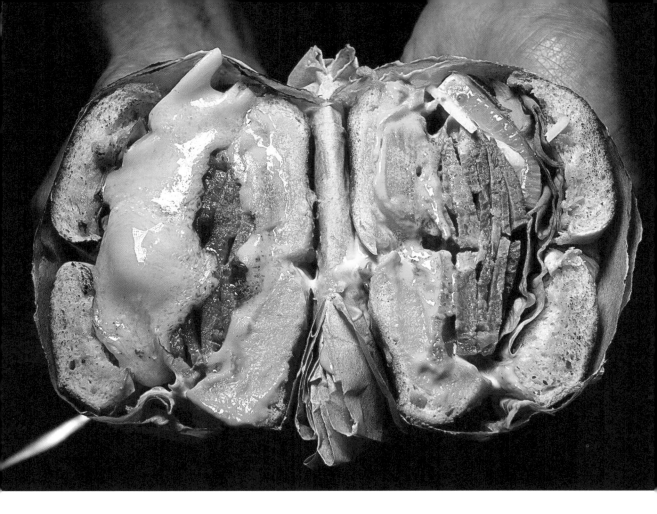

SAN FRANCISCO SALT BEEF
DELI BAGEL

1 BAGEL

The infamous San Francisco bagel, smothered in vintage Cheddar, melted over the original salt beef, with mustard and dill pickle. Yep, this is the real thing right here, cheesemeisters! You'll need to find the salt beef recipe in here and wait five long days to taste it, but you can bet yo' bottom dollar it'll be worth it. Wrapped in greaseproof and simply carved in half?! Well, boil my bagel!

77

EQUIPMENT:

Greaseproof paper

Sharp knife

Mighty appetite

INGREDIENTS:

San Francisco-style bagel – most supermarkets do them

Hunk of salt beef from my recipe

Burger mustard

Mayonnaise

Smokey BBQ sauce

1 beef tomato

A few thin slices of raw onion

Some lettuce – just for colour!

Dill pickle – gherkins – large ones in a jar

Vintage Cheddar cheese – sliced or grated

METHOD:

Throw the lettuce in the bin and start this recipe!

Heat up the grill and slide the tray one notch down from normal. Wait until hot.

Slide the whole bagel under the hot grill and lightly toast on both sides. Only then do you slice the crispy Bagel into a top and a bottom. Put the top to one side.

With the mustard, give a few swirls on the bottom of the bagel, followed by mayo and BBQ sauce. Top this with raw onion and a beef tomato slice and gherkin. Top this with 8 very thin slices of the salt beef.

Nearly there now.

Top the beef with the Cheddar and slide back under the grill to melt the cheese. This happens quickly, so keep an eye on it. Top the melted cheese with the lettuce and then the top of the bagel.

Sit the filled bagel to one side and rip off some greaseproof paper, big enough to wrap this whopper. Wrap up the bagel USA-style, nice and tight. Slice through the middle, stopping just before the bottom, so as not to cut the bottom of the greaseproof, and split apart.

Revealing the real San Francisco delight beneath.

DELICATESSEN FOOD

NEW YORK REUBEN SANDWICH

FOR ONE VERY BIG APPETITE

Associated with New York's kosher delis, this leviathan sandwich is an awesome task to eat – although not strictly kosher as it combines a pile of salt beef and cheese on there. Nonetheless you know you've arrived stateside when you order one of these grilled rye bread Reuben sandwiches. According to Omaha folklore, the Reuben was first served up to a late-night poker session by Reuben Kulakovsky, a local grocer. Charles Schimmel, one of the players, loved it so much he whacked it on the menu at his 'Plush Horse' hotel restaurant. However, there is a competing claim from Arnold Reuben of New York City, who claims there was a similar sandwich served at one of his Reuben's restaurants, but that is only substantiated by family recollections, so the claim is pretty weak in my book. This is the king of salt beef sandwiches, whoever lays claim to it, and you can now make your own!

You will need a sandwich maker for this, I think. I used a grill for the photograph, but a sandwich maker will keep the sandwich together while it grills.

You'll work it out somehow.

For one, but can serve two!

INGREDIENTS:

Rye bread – I make my own, but there are plenty of shop-bought versions

200g good quality deli salt beef

Sauerkraut

Fresh basil – to your taste

Sharp Cheddar – grated

Russian dressing, or ketchup, or mustard and mayo mixed together

Butter

METHOD:

Lightly butter your 2 slices of rye bread (this will be the bottom and top of the sandwich). Spread the non-buttered side with Russian dressing or the suggested equivalent. On of the bottom slice, layer the fresh basil and 10–12 slices of super-thin corned beef. Top with lots of sauerkraut and finally the sharp, grated Cheddar. Put on the lid (butter side to the top) and press down to join all the ingredients. Whack it onto your sandwich grill until unctuous!

If grilling, you will have to turn it halfway through.

Either way, grill it within an inch of its life.

Runny, cheesy, meaty, piquant, grilled heaven!

CHEDDAR AND HAM CROISSANT

MAKES 10-12 CROISSANTS

I have always been a keen Francophile and a keen baker, so the need to try out my own croissant was a quest I just had to do. Croissants are correctly named 'French Viennoiserie Pastries' as they originate from Vienna. They are made with a yeast-leavened dough that has been laminated with butter, in multiple layers. This recipe holds a lot of good patisserie memories for me, as I struggled through with the determination needed to crack the code on these puff pastry delights. To make croissants takes two days, but the sections split down relatively easily if you follow the recipe with some care. Patience will deliver multi-layered (32 in this case) croissants that give a light outer crunch and then slowly collapse on the tongue. This is a delight in itself, but the key here is when the tongue hits the savoury ham and Cheddar. You can modify this recipe to add golden marzipan if you wish, which just transforms coffee time! Or indeed you could substitute the cheese and ham with myriad fillings. A methodical baker's approach here pays dividends and brings us very close to topping a shop-bought French alternative. I think they're better because they're straight from the oven and you get the immediacy of the warm buttery aroma as you bite into them.

Although two days sounds like a chore, the actual time spent with the dough is about 45 minutes from start to finish.

EQUIPMENT:

Bread mixing bowl

Rolling pin

Baking/greaseproof paper

Scissors

Knife

Straight edge or bread scraper

2 baking sheets

Zipper bags (optional)

Cling wrap

Warmed bread mixing bowl – just warmed in the oven is an ideal starting point

INGREDIENTS:

250g warm water

12g dried active yeast

1 tsp castor sugar

300g bread flour

150g plain flour

1 tsp salt

40g castor sugar

50g unsalted butter – at room temperature (I use artisan French butter, available from good supermarkets)

250g of slightly salted butter for the laminating

METHOD:

Day 1

Pour the warm water into your warmed bowl.

Add the teaspoon of sugar and then the yeast. Gently incorporate with your fingers – nice and gently. Leave for 10 minutes to fizz – if there is no fizz at this point, your yeast is old and will need to be replaced with fresher yeast.

When you have a good yeast fizz, add all the flour, salt, 40g of sugar and room-temperature-butter and mix with your hands until you have a dough.

Knead this dough on your work surface for 5–8 minutes until smooth but still a little sticky.

I add sprinkled flour (either bread or plain) in small doses for this knead, but it can take about 3 tablespoons depending on the conditions on the day. Remember, smooth with a tacky surface that just sticks to your fingers.

This kneading is the last time you can manipulate your dough, so put some effort into making it smooth.

Put the dough back in your bowl and cover (in an oven in winter, or just left to rise in summer) and 'bulk rise' for 3 hours. Then store overnight in the fridge to enhance the flavour.

Day 2

Two hours before you resume work on the croissants, take the 250g pat of butter from the fridge to allow it to reach an ambient temperature. You want it to be malleable but not room temperature.

Once at a malleable temperature, rub the pat of butter in some flour and then sandwich between two sheets of baking paper. Then, roll it out with a rolling pin into a 20x30cm rectangle. You will need to start the rolling process by lightly hitting the butter with the rolling pin and making sure your greaseproof is large enough to take a 20x30cm rectangle.

Put the 'sandwiched' butter in the fridge to toughen a little.

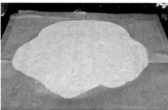

But not too much as we don't want it to be brittle.

You are aiming for the butter and the cold dough to be of similar consistency, which is important.

THE LAMINATION.

Laminating is a baking term for making puff pastry. It is the process of skilfully keeping the butter and dough at the same consistency throughout your 3 turns of folding and rolling. It is an art form, but easy to get to grips with if you use care.

No brittle butter here, cheesemeisters!

Take both the butter and the dough from the fridge.

Tip out the dough onto a flour-dusted work surface and roll into a large rectangle 50x45cm.

Lay the butter in the middle of the dough. This will leave you with a substantial overlap, so that you can tuck in top, bottom and sides to fully cover the butter.

Now gently roll the dough/butter to tease them together and disperse the butter to 'fit' the dough.

Now your efforts should be assured and swift, but gentle.

Roll the dough/butter lengthways to approximately 50cm in length.

Then fold the top to two-thirds of the way down the dough and fold up the bottom third to reach the top of your first fold, creating a three-fold rectangle. This movement is critical.

Cover with cling wrap and refrigerate for 30 minutes to toughen up the butter.

Take from the fridge and remove the cling wrap. Have the rectangle of dough in front of you with the longest edge nearest you. Turn the packet 90° to then have the shortest edge nearest you. Sprinkle some flour and roll the dough away from you to 50cm again and repeat the three folds.

Cover again in cling wrap and refrigerate if required, but don't if the butter is quite brittle.

Repeat the process by turning 90° and rolling again, keeping your eye on the consistency of the butter inside. If softening, refrigerate for half an hour, but if brittle leave to warm a little. It's a balancing act.

You have now created the puff pastry element of the croissant – well done.

MAKING THE CROISSANT:

Take the dough/butter from the fridge.

Cut your Cheddar into cuboids – (chip-shaped) of 8cm x 8mm x 8mm and wrap the cuboids in ham.

On a well-dusted surface, roll out the dough (20cm wide and approximately 70cm long) with the longest edge nearest you, making sure you roll it to just under a pound coin in thickness.

Take a straight edge and a knife to cut your croissants into triangles (approximately 20cm long and 10cm across the bottom width). This should make 10–12 consecutive triangles.

Place the Cheddar/ham rolls on the 10cm edge and roll to the point of the triangle, making the classic croissant shape.

Place the croissants on a floured baking tray, trapping the tip of the triangle underneath, and then repeat with rest of your batch.

Cover each baking sheet with cling wrap so that it lightly holds the croissants.

Let them rest to rise slightly, for 2–3 hours – they will puff up a little.

Preheat your oven to 170°C. Glaze the croissants with egg wash and bake for 20–25 minutes until golden and fragrant.

OR

You can cook two now and refrigerate or freeze the rest.

If freezing, put them in twos in zipper bags.

They will keep for up to a month in the freezer, or for a week in the fridge on the baking sheet and covered with cling wrap.

These croissants are special.

You can also change the fillings to marzipan, rolled into long thin strips and placed down the centre line, top to bottom, and rolled as per the above instructions into your croissants; or sprinkle cinnamon over the finished and glazed croissants before baking.

All are truly awesome!

Enjoy!

PORK, PICKLE AND VINTAGE CHEDDAR PIE

MAKES 4 PIES

A great pork pie is a pie whose pastry surface audibly cracks under the pressure of your knife, and it has a salty, savoury jelly, enveloping the nicely dense filling – these are the criteria of a classic pork pie. If any pie had umami it should be the humble pork pie. Three layers of excellence are what the pie is trying to deliver as you take that first bite. Alas, the modern supply chain has slowly decelerated the class in the pork pie, a tragedy for our very British pie industry and is another regrettable reflection on processing. If the great PP is your preference then we are on the same page (quite literally). I have put effort in here to tick all the boxes above and some. I have been meticulous in creating just the right shortening in the pastry by adding some Cheddar to the lard, adding shortening and flavour. We are using strong flavoured chicken stock for the jelly and we are using smoked bacon and vintage Cheddar in the mince filling, accompanied by a homemade pickle in the centre. All the above criteria are present and correct, making this pie perfect for an al fresco lunch or a picnic, with a crunchy salad drizzled in smooth vinaigrette, or a Christmas offering for all the family, or as a bit of a show-off with friends. One thing is for sure, you will have made the perfect pork pie and you'll be a lot more judgemental when faced with the pale imposters from the high street or supermarket.

EQUIPMENT:

Bowl to mix the filling

Pan for the shortening

Pan for the jelly

4 22x3cm non-stick pie moulds – slotted

Rolling pin

Funnel

Pastry brush and cup for glaze

Baking tray to catch juices in the oven

Pouring jug – for the jelly

INGREDIENTS:

Filling:

700g mince – 70/30 mix of pork and smoked bacon

15g powdered mustard

6g salt

Nutmeg

1 pickle per pie

70g vintage Cheddar

Lots of freshly ground black pepper

4 x 5mm slices of Cheddar – for top of pie

Hot Water Pastry:

400g plain flour

120g lard

60g Cheddar

200g water

Egg for glaze

Jelly:

250g chicken stock

Salt

6 gelatine leaves

METHOD:

First make the pastry by putting all shortening ingredients – lard, water, Cheddar – into the pan and bring to the boil. Once boiling, take off the heat and reserve.

In your mixing bowl, weigh out the flour, add half a teaspoon of salt, and pour into the hot shortening. Mix with the end of a wooden spoon to distribute the heat, before handling to bring the pastry together, so it comes away from the bowl and leaves very little behind. You may need a tad more water to soften if too dry, or flour if too wet. It should be pliable in your hands and look like a good pastry. Once you have this pastry, wrap in cling wrap and leave to cool and harden a little – either in the fridge for half an hour or in a cool place.

Next make your filling and jelly.

For the jelly, slide your gelatine leaves into cold water for 5 minutes to soften. Once softened, add to your pan of chicken stock, bring to the boil and season with salt, thus melting the gelatine. Take from the heat and allow to cool to room temperature.

For the filling, throw your mince into the bowl, add the mustard and a good few gratings of nutmeg. Grate in the Cheddar and season with 5g of salt and lots of grindings of pepper.

You will need some Cheddar for the top of the pie too, so bear that in mind.

You now have everything ready to make your pies.

You should have 680g in total of pastry. Split into 4 x 170g pieces. Each piece will make a top and a bottom for each pie. Take one piece and cover the remainder.

Cut this piece in half and choose one for the bottom. You will need to butter the pie moulds now. Roll out the bottom to fit the size of the pie mould. Push into the mould carefully. Roll out the top of your pie (same size as before) and set aside. Set up your egg glaze in a cup – by whisking vigorously with a fork – and your pastry brush.

Take 160g of filling and roll into a ball. Slide a pickle into the middle, keeping an eye on 'right side up' to help with presentation. Wrap the mince around the pickle and offer the filling up to the pie and lay in the centre. Slide the Cheddar slice on top of the mince and add a few grindings of pepper. Now paint some glaze around the edges of the bottom pastry. Slide on the top of the pie and press around the edges to secure top to bottom. I now crimp my pies with a pinching motion, to create a series of crimps around the edge. Only now do I trim the pastry around the pie by carefully

lifting the pie and slicing off the excess pastry with a vertical knife, feeling for the edge of the mould to guide you.

Glaze the top of the pie with your pastry brush and allow it to dry by setting it aside. Repeat with all four pies.

Make a hole in the centre of each pie. This is where the funnel will be inserted at a later stage, but will also allow steam to escape from the cooking pie.

Place on the roasting tray and slide into the preheated oven and cook for 1 hour. Have some kitchen foil to hand, if the tops cook too quickly, to protect the tops from over colouring. After 40 minutes, take the pies out of the oven. Carefully slide them back in separately onto the oven wire shelf and place the tray on the bottom of the oven to continue catching juices. This allows the bottom of the pies to cook through. After the hour, take out of the oven and rest on a baking rack, if possible, until cooled to room temperature.

Now we need to fill the pies with jelly. You may need to reheat the jelly to loosen the grip of the gelatine at this point. Just lightly bring up the heat, whilst stirring. Once the gelatine loosens, remove from the heat. Pour some warmed jelly mix into a pouring jug.

With the funnel in place – in the hole of the pie – lightly try pouring the jelly into the funnel. Pour and wait for it to work its way into the pie. Repeat with all four pies and carefully refrigerate until 'fridge cold'.

You now have four fine artisan pork pies.

Enjoy every bite of umami.

BLCT

BACON, LETTUCE, CHEESE, TOMATO

I think I can take this opportunity to come out as a BLCT lover. It's been a hard road to get to this place. I almost blurt it out in the sandwich shop, but just as I open my mouth, something benign and random comes out and everyone thinks I'm a bit weird. As if. To add to the BLT is impossible, isn't it? But can I just say that, if you've had the delights of a bacon and cheese toasted sandwich, then this secret addition of mine seems a little less shocking. In my opinion the BLT is just a little tame and will never hang from the chandelier with a dry Martini in hand. This is where the addition of cheese takes us. To the naughty step for me to think about what I've said before I can come back. Yes, it's that naughty. It's not for the dieter, and once eaten you'll probably have to skip a couple of meals, but at least you can rejoice in the knowledge that a BLCT lover is a forever lover – never to return once you've traversed the prison wall of tradition.

EQUIPMENT:

A good grill
Swiss roll baking tray
Grater

INGREDIENTS:

3 rashers of smoked back bacon per
   person – from the butcher
50g good vintage Cheddar – grated
1–2 ripe vine tomatoes per person – thickly
   sliced
Handful of mixed lettuce and leaves
Great tomato ketchup
Great choice of bread – sourdough for me

METHOD:

Turn on the grill to high and lay your chosen slices of bread on the Swiss roll baking tray and toast lightly. Take the bread off the baking tray carefully and replace the toast with the back bacon and grill until cooked. Take the baking tray out from under the grill and tip the bacon juices onto the inside edge of both slices of toast, then place the bacon on the bottom slice. Grate the vintage Cheddar over the bacon and slip back under the grill to melt the cheese into a cheese-on-toast appearance. Take out from under the grill again and add the thickly sliced tomatoes and slip back under the grill to cook and colour the tomatoes. Carefully take from the grill again and smear tomato ketchup thickly over the top slice of bread. Sprinkle a good handful of mixed leaves over the tomatoes and sprinkle with fresh ground black pepper. Top the sandwich with the toasted top and pierce with a knife to hold together.

You have now joined the BLCT club – you know it makes sense.

Run Forrest, Run!

THE KING OF SANDWICHES (V)

If there was ever a sandwich that moves me with memories of childhood and early working life, and indeed still comes into my memory banks from time to time, giving me the urge to make one straight away, then this is it. The king of sandwiches is a fresh oven bottom muffin with cheese and piccalilli on – a good dose of piccalilli is key. This sandwich when made properly will give me a cold sweat on my forehead and only then will I be satisfied by its quality. The cheese sandwich is the staple of many a manual worker for lunch or a hiker for sustenance or a train driver for concentration energy. We can all identify with the cheese butty. Crucial to this beauty is the oven bottom muffin, which we are going to scratch make. Originating in the North near Oldham, the 'backstone' muffin was finished on a quarry backstone that had sat in the oven for hours, thus creating the near burnt top from contact with the hot stone, Only fresh for a day, this muffin was the mainstay of my childhood. I have been known to throw on the KitchenAid in the early morning and by 10 o'clock have fresh backstones for our delectation. Northern umami on a butty.

EQUIPMENT:

Mixing bowl for bread – or a KitchenAid

Scales

2 baking sheets – lightly floured

Cling wrap

Measuring jug

24cm frying pan

Pair of tongs – for lifting the hot muffins

White pepper

INGREDIENTS:

400g bread flour

7g active dried yeast

1 tbsp butter – softened and cubed

2 tbsp sunflower oil

180ml warm water

90ml milk

1 tsp salt

1 tsp sugar

Great Cheddar of your choice

Your favourite piccalilli – I make my own

METHOD:

With the mixing bowl on the scales weigh out the flour and yeast. Add the salt and sugar. Add the butter and sunflower oil. Mix the contents until you have the breadcrumb consistency needed. Slowly add the liquid – water and milk – until the mixture comes together as a dough and cleans the sides of the bowl – sometimes you may not need all the liquid. Knead for 5 minutes on the work surface or in the KitchenAid. Shape into a rough ball and cover with cling wrap. Leave in a warm place for an hour or more until doubled in size.

Take out of the bowl and make a sausage shape of the dough. Cut into 8 equal parts and work with one at a time. With the dough in your hand, and holding either side between thumb and first finger, pull the "skin" of the dough away and around the outside of the dough, all the way to the bottom, thus tightening and smoothing the top of your muffin. Then it's time to roll the dough on your lightly floured work surface into a round muffin about 12cm wide. Lay this muffin on a baking sheet and repeat with the other 7 muffins. Lightly cover each tray with cling wrap and leave somewhere warm for 30 minutes to prove.

Preheat the oven to 180°C.

Once proved, uncover the muffins and press a finger into the middle of each one. Slide them into the preheated oven for 7 minutes per side.

In the meantime, have a dry frying pan on the hob at a medium heat – to heat it up for later. Once the muffins have come out of the oven, take the tongs and carefully lay one at a time, face down, on the hot frying pan to colour the tops. I let them colour a lot – nearly burnt – but you should choose what suits you.

Eat these muffins through the day – they will be stale tomorrow, but they make a handsome sandwich.

Then it's a case of carving some fine Cheddar and making the base of your sandwich. Top with a good daub of piccalilli and put on the top – you must now push down hard with the palm of your hand to press the sandwich into shape.

Perfect!

CHEDDAR AND FENNEL BREAD (V)

I have been making bread for many years and have my own sourdough starter, Oscar. We have both come a long way, but I thought for this recipe I would let him step aside for a simpler savoury loaf that we can all make. The addition of Cheddar and fennel is key here, the soft anise flavour melding with the creamy Cheddar taste is the clever twist. Totally artisanal bread is a healthy life benefit, as you know exactly what is in there and are therefore not eating any unknown processed ingredients. For me artisan bread-making is about a calm kitchen, just coolly pottering around, bringing the simple ingredients together. The pay-off being the aromas from the oven and the crispy crust when you first slice a warm and real loaf – not forgetting the amazing toast from this bread! All these elements are here in this time-friendly recipe. The added bonus is, with good aftercare, this loaf can last you up to a week.

EQUIPMENT:
Good pot or earthenware bread bowl
Lidded stainless pan, 21x11cm
Greaseproof paper
KitchenAid with dough hook – optional
Baking sheet, 25x36cm
Shower cap

INGREDIENTS:
300g plain flour
200g wholemeal or rye flour
350ml hand-warm water
10g salt
8g dried active yeast
10g fennel seeds
100g grated Cheddar

METHOD:

If it is a lovely summer day, you will have a great ambient temperature in the kitchen for bread-making, while in the winter it is best to use the oven to create the same ambient temperature.

Turn your oven to 100°C and put your bread bowl in to warm up for 5 minutes. In the meantime, weigh out your flours, yeast and salt. Turn the oven off before removing the bowl and throwing in the combined ingredients, into either the KitchenAid bowl or the warmed bread bowl.

If using KitchenAid, lock in place and use speed 1.

Stir to combine the dry ingredients before slowly adding the warm water, whilst stirring to create a dough. Work this dough in the bowl or KitchenAid for a couple of minutes to decide if the dough is the right consistency. Add more water if too dry, or more flour if too wet, until the dough is malleable and looks nice. Now add the fennel seeds and grated Cheddar. Work them into the dough for a minute.

Now you have a dough that can be kneaded on a lightly floured work surface or KitchenAid. Knead for 8 minutes until smooth and elastic. If you press a finger into the dough it should bounce back with some vitality. Not all the way back, but just three quarters of the way back is a good sign.

Put back into bread bowl or unlock the KitchenAid bowl, cover with a shower cap (Yes, a shower cap!) and put back into the (turned-off) oven for the first rise – 1 hour.

Take from the oven when the dough is doubled in size. Now is the time to 'knock back' the dough on a lightly floured work surface. Basically you are knocking out the air from the first rise – not completely though. I knock it back for 10 seconds. I then shape the loaf into its final shape.

Holding the dough in your hands, roughly shape into a sphere before putting it onto your lightly floured work surface. With your hands either side of the dough, at 9 o'clock and 3 o'clock, turn your palms to the ceiling. With a cupping motion, you will now push your flat hands towards each other but under the dough, whilst pushing the 'skin' of the dough underneath. Turn the dough 90° and push the skin underneath with the same motion again. Repeat in this manner until the 'skin' of the dough is nice and tight, but not ripped – this would be too much.

Rip off a 40cm square of greaseproof paper. In the middle of each edge of the square make a 10cm rip towards the middle of the square. You should have four rips pointing towards the middle. Lightly flour the surface of the paper and gently lift your dough with flat hands from either side again and lay it onto the middle of the floured paper. Now, very gently (cradle-like) lift this paper and dough onto a baking sheet (25x36cm) that will take the finished loaf. Lightly flour the top of the loaf with the wholemeal or rye flour and lay a length of cling film over the top and very lightly cover the dough. Lay in a warm place or the cooled oven for the second rise – 30 minutes.

Once slightly risen, take from oven (if using) and set oven to 220°C. Put the lidded stainless pan in the oven and wait for the temperature to rise. When fully heated, carefully take the (red-hot) pan from the oven.

With a sharp knife, cut four slashes in the top of the dough to make a square, where each slash is 1cm deep and each slash touches the other.

Take off the red-hot lid and cradle-lift the greaseproof paper and dough into the stainless pan – it should snugly fit in there. Put on the lid, but don't worry about the greaseproof paper sticking out from the lid.

Put back in the hot oven, covered, for 22 minutes.

Carefully remove from the oven and take off the lid. The loaf should have risen nicely towards the top of the pan and is ready to colour. Change the oven temperature to 180°C and carefully place back into the oven, unlidded, for a further 22 minutes, or to the right colour for you.

ANTIGUAN BUN AND CHEESE (V)

This small Caribbean island of 365 white sandy beaches is a proud nation of food lovers. These people will tuck into bright vibrant food. Fish is a staple, with conch and salt fish prominent in their cuisine. Antiguans also have a sweet tooth and this recipe is the epitome of the Antiguan way of enjoying cheese in a sweet bun. Very much everyday bread, this bun follows the sweet line with a good amount of sugar, combined with raisins, steeped in spices and citrus peel. So the Antiguan will have a bun, filled with cheese as a wrap-up for lunch. They usually only have an American processed slice to choose from at home, but here we add what we want – and that will be a creamy, crunchy Cheddar to match the sweet spiciness of this unique bread.

EQUIPMENT:

Bread mixing bowl or a KitchenAid
   with bread hook
Mixing bowl
Wooden spoon

Measuring jug
2 baking trays
Pastry brush – for glazing buns
Cling wrap
Kitchen roll

INGREDIENTS:

Main mix:

100g raisins – soaked in warm water

Spices – ½ tsp each of cinnamon, nutmeg and a palmful of orange peel from a zester

260g plain flour

1 tbsp of golden castor sugar

½ tsp salt

30g butter - melted

Yeast Mix:

2 tbsp plain flour

1 tbsp sugar

1 level tsp dried active yeast

125g warm tap water

1 egg

Plus:

1 egg for glazing

METHOD:

We'll be using 2 mixes for this recipe that will combine after 5 minutes.

First, in your bowl mix the 125g water, 2 tbsp flour, yeast, sugar and mix through. Leave for 5 minutes to fizz.

In the meantime, prepare the KitchenAid/bread bowl with the dry ingredients.

In goes the 260g of plain flour, followed by the remaining 1 tbsp of sugar and the salt.

Drain the raisins now and dry them on kitchen roll, then set aside.

Mix these dry ingredients briefly to combine and then add the yeast mix and the egg. Mix thoroughly, add the melted butter and raisins now to mix into a dough. No1 speed on the KitchenAid or by hand, knead the dough for 7 minutes until smooth and not sticky at all. It will have a smooth shine but no 'stick'.

Place in your bread bowl or KitchenAid bowl, cover and leave in a warm place for an hour or so to double in size.

Once doubled, take from the bowl and (on an un-floured surface) fashion into a thick sausage shape by loosely rolling your hands over the top. Split into 4 equal pieces with a knife – keep three to one side and work on the one left.

Take the dough to hand and think about tightening the 'skin' of the dough. I put my thumbs on top and entice it, thus tightening the 'skin' towards the underside – left thumb going left and right thumb going right. Turn over now so the underside is uppermost. Hold in your left hand and use your right hand to continually pinch the 'skin' into a dumpling shape. You should feel the 'skin' tightening now, while you pinch the dough into the middle.

Lightly flour the baking sheets and lay the first bun on there, with the smoothest side up. Repeat until all the buns are done. Cover loosely over the top with cling wrap and leave for the second rise – half an hour in a warm place. They will grow into a good bun size.

Set the oven to 180°C.

Break the egg into a cup and paint the surface of each bun to coat with a glaze.

Slide the baking trays into the oven for 20 minutes, keeping an eye on the colour.

When happy with the colour and timing, take from the oven and allow to cool on a rack for half an hour.

Enjoy!

KÄSEBROT (V)

The Germans eat more bread than any other country in the world and therefore their bread is said to be the best in the world. Bread sustains the German culture and according to the bread register of the German Institute of Bread (Yes, they really do have one) there are now more than 3,200 officially recognised types of bread in the country. For breakfast, lunch and dinner (or abendbrot, literally 'bread of the evening'). Safe to say that the addition of cheese into their bread was a no-brainer, hence the name Käsebrot – cheesebread. This bread is easy to construct and rewards the time invested, waiting for the two-stage rise of the dough. The payback is the drift of bread and cheese aromas throughout the house as it cooks and we all love a good payback from a recipe. I have substituted the German cheese for Cheddar and therein I have stumbled upon a recipe that should slide into the awesome category very easily. There is also the extra benefit of it making a fine toast; I see a nice chunky slice of clothbound, aged Cheddar and a pickle, but it's a free-for-all on the toppings, of course.

EQUIPMENT:

Bread mixing bowl
Bowl for measuring weight
Small pan for the milk
Sieve

Scales
Wooden spoon
Spring form tin with a loose
   bottom – 20x6cm

INGREDIENTS:

14g dried active yeast

100ml whole milk

1 tbsp sugar

1 tsp salt

1 egg

120g vintage Cheddar – grated

250g plain flour – sifted

METHOD:

Warm your mixing bowl in the oven for 4 minutes. When it's nice and warm, turn off the oven and close the door, for later. Weigh the yeast and throw into the bowl. Add 3 tbsp of water and let it fizz for 5 minutes.

In the pan add the measured milk and add the sugar and salt. Raise the heat to dissolve the crystals and take off the heat immediately and cool a little.

Measure out the flour in a bowl and have a sieve ready to sift the flour.

Once cooled, pour the milk mixture into the yeast, crack in the egg and sift half of the flour. Mix well with the wooden spoon and then add the remaining half of flour in two quarters, whilst mixing. Add the grated cheese here and mix. You may need to adjust the water content with warm water. You will have a ball of dough that will now be worked into bread dough.

Take from the bowl and knead for 5 minutes on a lightly floured work surface until the dough doesn't stick to the surface. Work so the dough is smooth and when pressed with the finger it partially springs back – perfect.

Push a dimple in the top of the dough and fill it with olive oil. Use this olive oil to cover the dough.

Put back in the bowl and cover with cling wrap or similar and place back into the just warm oven from heating the bowl. Allow to double in size over the next 2 hours. You may need to blip the oven from time to time just to keep it from being cold.

After 2 hours it will have doubled and be ready for stage 2. Take the dough from the bowl and knock out all the air from stage 1.

Very lightly oil and then flour the spring form tin, then set aside.

With a cupping motion, and with both hands, cup and entice the dough underneath the dough, thus tightening the 'skin' of the dough on top. Turn 90° and cup and entice again. Repeat for 5 spins of 90°. You will now have a ball of dough. Press the flat of your hand on the ball and lightly press the top to just flatten the ball a little – pushing the ball out just an inch. Place the dough in the middle of the prepared spring form tin and push a dimple in the top of the dough. Fill this dimple with olive oil and then use that oil to cover the whole of the bread that is showing. Cover with cling wrap and place back in the warm oven for about an hour, for the second rise.

It will rise to the top of the tin and fill all areas.

Take from the oven and then preset the oven to 200°C.

Once the oven is at heat, take off the cling wrap and slide the uncovered tin into the middle of the oven for 20 minutes or until beautifully golden brown and smelling of lovely cheese. Take from the oven and let it cool for 5 minutes in the tin, before undoing the spring – which will just slide off the top – and entice the loose bottom free of the loaf.

Cool the opened loaf on a rack.

This bread is awesome toasted, by the way …

Enjoy!

ECCLES CAKES – DEAD FLY PIE

MAKES 8–10

The Eccles cake or the dead fly pie is similar to a turnover (but better) and clearly originates from the outskirts of Manchester and the district of Eccles. The word 'Eccles' means 'church', so I guess the cake was originated with the church congregation in mind. Through research I find that a certain Elizabeth Ratfield is

possibly the lady who invented them in 1793, when religion was a way of life and anything connected with the church was revered. So the 'church cake' was born. Maybe for après-service fare with tea and a chat with the vicar – the size of these cakes is key to that theory. Manchester has ownership to just a few culinary relics and Eccles cakes are probably the most available across the nation and abroad. We have the Manchester sausage (gorgeous), Vimto and Eccles cakes to our name and we hold them with pride. I have been making scratch Eccles cakes for years now and my only reservation has been that the currants fall all around as you very carefully consume them, but the addition of fine Cheddar becomes the glue to bind it all together. So, instead of eating Eccles cakes with cheese, which is customary, we are adding cheese to the filling ingredients – leaving you a spare hand to bid the vicar goodbye, of course.

EQUIPMENT:

Swiss roll baking tray

Mixing bowl

Zester

Small pan – to melt butter

Circular template with a 13cm diameter – a plate or something similar

Plain flour for dusting

pastry brush

INGREDIENTS:

1 pre-bought puff pastry weighing 500g

280g small currants

30g butter – melted

Zest of 1 orange

A good few shakes of ground cinnamon

60g sugar

70g sharp Cheddar – grated

Beaten egg

METHOD:

In your mixing bowl, combine the currants with the zested orange peel and sugar. Mix through the fingers to combine. Add the grated Cheddar and repeat the combining. Add the cinnamon and the melted butter to make a final mix with your fingers. Set aside.

Preheat your oven to 180°C.

With the puff pastry, flour the work surface and roll out to a thickness of a £1 coin, or thereabouts – I like a little less, but not much. Cut around your template, forming 8 circles of puff pastry – taking away the excess (which you can roll again and make a further 2). Have the beaten egg handy in a cup and a pastry brush.

It's time to construct these cakes. With one of the circles in front of you, fill the circle with a tbsp of currants. You need to gauge the right amount: by over-filling, the currants will spill off the pastry; by under-filling, you will have lots of spare pastry. Lift the edges of the circle and gather all the edges at the top, thus making a sack or cradle for the currants. Squeeze the join together at the top so it looks like a dumpling and completely encloses the filling ingredients, with no holes. Turn upside down and flatten with the palm of your hand and you can just see the currants under the thin pastry on top.

Slide all the cakes onto a floured Swiss roll tray and then into the oven for approximately 12 minutes until golden and clearly ready. Bring out of the oven and allow to cool to room temperature.

A right gradely addition to the coffee break.

HIGH-RISE SMOKED CHEDDAR SCONES (V)

MAKES 12 OR HALVE THE RECIPE FOR 6

When it comes to scones there is the multi-lateral conundrum of cream first or jam first? Many a cookbook has been filled with this mysterious, and can I say, most English enigma. The easy answer to that, cheesemeisters, is yes, you've guessed it, neither – just slam on the cheese and a good pickle. 'Hear! Hear!' you exclaim, oh dedicated cheese fiend! All agreed there then. These wee beauties are made with Montgomery smoked Cheddar and Wyke Farms' 'Ivy's Vintage', both fine examples of damn fine Cheddar, and I thought we would team them up for this most Somerset of scones. I don't think you'll find many fig farms around Somerset, but that's by the by where I come from. It's all in the crunch of the cheese and the figs, an extra dimension that works a treat here, methinks. The quantities here are for 12 scones and that is what I recommend, as they are rather moreish.

What's the fastest cake? Yep, scone.

And they will.

EQUIPMENT:

Mixing bowl

Scales

Grater

Rolling pin

2 baking trays

Sieve

Scone or biscuit
    cutter

Pastry brush

INGREDIENTS:

360g plain flour – sifted

4 tsp baking powder

50g castor sugar

4 soft (dried) figs – chopped

100g Cheddar – 50/50 mix of smoked and vintage

120ml buttermilk

A dash of cider – if needed

1 egg

Butter and your choice of jam

METHOD:

Set oven to 220°C.

First, sift the flour into your mixing bowl. Add the baking powder and castor sugar, stir to mix and then add the chopped figs. Grate the cheeses into the bowl and stir to combine equally. Make a hole in the centre of the mix and add the buttermilk and egg. Mix with a wooden spoon until the mixture comes together. If the mix needs more liquid to combine, add cider instead of water.

Lightly flour your work surface and lightly knead the dough for 15 seconds. With your rolling pin, roll the dough to about 2–3cm thick and keep nicely floured. Flour your baking sheets ready to take the scones.

With a scone or biscuit cutter, cut out your scones and place them on a baking tray, until full. You will have to pack the dough into a ball again and roll out, to continue cutting.

When you have exhausted the dough and made your 10–12 scones, take a beaten egg and brush the tops of each scone.

Slide into the oven for 12–14 minutes – you are looking for a lovely golden-brown appearance and a high-rise scone.

We like these with butter and apricot jam – the salt and sweet mix really works here.

Enjoy!

CHEDDAR-LOADED
SALT AND PEPPER CHIPS (V)

SERVES 2

Here we have the enigma of flavouring chips. I personally find it difficult to resist the salt and pepper flavour anyway, so I'm automatically drawn towards the addition of great extra mature Cheddar, spice and chips. Yes the chip has met its transport into the 21st century. Tossed in a wok with onions, peppers and chilli is a major step in the right direction for the humble chip. To then have Cheddar grated and melted over the top is taking it stratospheric and the chip will survive well with this kind of imaginative twist. I will just have to remind you though that this pursuit is best conducted at home, where you know the ingredients and can choose how spicy to make them and, most importantly, you can add fine Cheddar and not any old mass-produced, oil-ridden imitation. To cook this dish at home pays massive dividends. This recipe rocks the chip world!

EQUIPMENT: Roasting tray, wok, wooden spatula

INGREDIENTS:

Chips:

3–4 medium potatoes – (Maris Pipers are good) unpeeled and chunky cut

1 medium onion – unpeeled and halved lengthways

1–2 tbsp groundnut or olive oil

Wok:

1 medium onion – halved and sliced

3 cloves garlic – chopped

1 pepper (any colour but good and fresh) – halved and thickly sliced

Red chilli – seeded and chopped

Or chilli flakes to your taste

Juice of 1 lime

Salt and freshly ground pepper

60g Cheddar – grated

METHOD:

Heat the oven to 180°C. Wash and chunky cut your chips from the unpeeled potatoes. Throw them into the roasting tray with the halved onion and drizzle with the chosen oil. Throw into the oven on the middle shelf and shake the tray every 15 minutes. Cook for 1 hour until browned and crispy. Set aside

In the meantime, oil up the wok with groundnut oil. When hot, throw in the sliced onion and garlic and spin around for a minute or so. Throw in the pepper and continue spinning them around for 2 minutes – still on a high heat. Throw in the chilli, salt and pepper – to taste.

Set grill to high

Add the already cooked and hot chips and spin all these ingredients together to create the familiar mix of salt and pepper chips. Give them a minute before adding a squeeze of lime.

Have your grill set to hot and throw the wok mix into the grill pan – without mesh – and grate over the Cheddar and rip the baked onion apart and throw in the mix too. Grill the mix until the cheese has melted.

Dish up the salt and pepper chips fast and devour them accordingly.

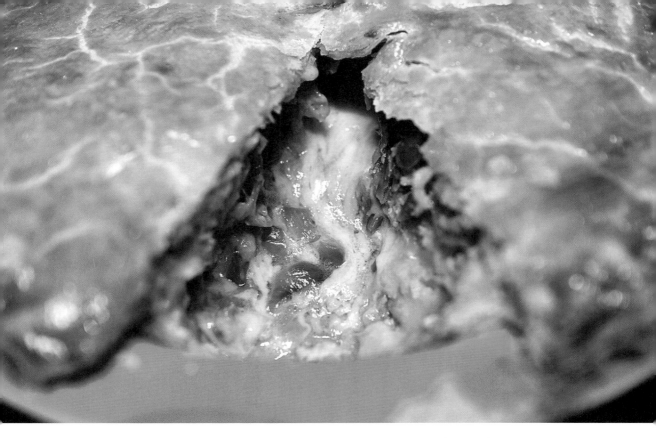

CHEDDAR AND SWEET ONION PIE

UP TO 8 SERVINGS

Let's rejoice that we have a superb cheese 'n' onion pie here. A pie that delivers from start to finish, insofar as we are throwing together a shortcrust pastry, nice and short and melting to the mouth. We have the onions slowly cooking and gathering caramelisation from the bottom of the pan, giving savoury/sweet notes around the house, followed by the aromas of pie as it cooks in the oven. The pie dish comes into its own here, a special dish made just for a nice deep pie. Pie is the ultimate comfort food and we need a good reliable and versatile pie dish to match up to the job. Size is the important factor here and I use a 24cm stoneware pie dish with 4cm depth and a lovely shiny glaze. I love this dish and it will last me many years, because I will look after it as if it were one of my family. There are myriad dishes out there and you will need to make your lifelong choice. You may already have your great dish and just want to get on with the recipe. So, here we go …

EQUIPMENT:

Large bowl for pastry and
    doubling up for the filling

24cm pie dish

Medium heavy-bottomed
    pan and lid

Large pan with lid

Rolling pin

Sharp knife

Measuring jug for eggs –
    fork for whipping

Pastry brush

Oven gloves

INGREDIENTS:

PASTRY:

300g plain flour

120g salted butter – cold from the fridge
    and chopped into 1cm cubes

Milk – up to 3 tbsp

FILLING:

3 large onions or 4 medium

Glug of olive oil and a knob of butter

200g Cheddar of your choice – cut into
    3cm chunks

2 medium potatoes – quartered and
    unpeeled

4 large eggs, plus another egg to glaze

Salt and white pepper

METHOD:

Peel and halve the onions, then slice with the grain into half moon slices of 2mm.

In your large pan, throw in the oil and butter and the sliced onions on a medium-high heat. Wait for the sizzle, turn down to number 2 and put on the lid. Every 15 minutes or so, check the pan and give it a swirl with a wooden spoon. You will be releasing some onion from the bottom that will be catching. This is what you want, as it will be colouring the onions to help with caramelisation. I cook them in this manner for about an hour. They are then golden and sweet smelling and ready for the pie. Set aside.

In the meantime you can make the pastry. In the bowl weigh out the flour and add the cubed butter. Using your hands, you need to break up the butter into the flour – keep 'rubbing' (lift and rub) with your fingertips – quickly mixing until you have an even breadcrumb consistency. Try and be quick here, so as not to melt the butter too much in your hands.

Once 'breadcrumbed', add the milk. This should be about 4 tbsp, but each pastry mix is different. Just add enough to bring the pastry nicely together into a ball, just so the ball of pastry is not wet, but remains cohesive and malleable. It is now ready for rolling. Many chefs say to wrap in cling film and refrigerate at this point, but I think it is very usable at room temperature.

In the other pan, cover the potatoes with water and cook until just tender – 15 minutes on a simmer. Drain and set aside.

Butter your pie dish, so all areas are lightly buttered, and set aside.

Flour your work surface and slowly start the rolling process of the pastry. Cut the pastry in half, one for the top and one for the bottom, and set one aside. It should have a good rolling consistency and it will give to light pressure from the pin. Keep the flour going down as you go, to lightly keep the surfaces floured. Roll out into a 33cm diameter circle and about a pound coin/3mm thickness.

When happy, you can start to construct the pie. Lay the rolling pin horizontally across the pastry circle from 11 o'clock to 1 o'clock. Roll the small part of the pastry above the pin onto the pin. Slowly roll the pin and pastry towards yourself, thus 'loading the pin' with pastry, until all the pastry is wrapped around the pin. Take over to the buttered pie dish and unroll the pastry circle to completely cover the dish, equally. Lightly press the pastry into the corners of the dish, whilst simultaneously lifting the outside of the pastry off the rim, thus allowing the pastry to be safely pushed into the corners. Let the outside of the pastry hang off the edge of the dish and take your sharp knife to trim off the edge, holding the dish in your left hand and cutting in a downwards motion, whilst slowly spinning the dish and also feeling the edge of the dish with the knife, making the trim nice and neat. This is a bit tricky but you will have seen your mother do this through time. Try and breathe too!

In a bowl, mix the cooled onions and potatoes with the Cheddar and give it a good mix to amalgamate the filling. Season with white pepper. Once you are happy, pour into the pie dish and rub around to distribute equally into a nice mound, just poking up above the rim of the dish. Crack the eggs into a bowl and whip up for 5 seconds to just split the yolk and a little more. Pour this over the pie and allow to distribute by tapping the pie dish on the work surface lightly and swirling the dish in your hands. With a fork, press the flat tines into the flat edge of the pie pastry, like the second markings on a clock. Dip your finger into some of the egg and rub around the edge to cover all the rim of the pie. Set aside.

Flour the work surface again and roll out the top of the pie in the same manner as the bottom – roughly, a 33cm circle – load the pin again as before and unroll the pastry equally to cover the whole pie and have an overhang.

With your thumb and first finger, pinch the rim of the pastry to essentially join the top of the pie to the bottom. Continue fully around the pie in this manner, pinching and moving, pinching and moving, until all neat and pinched around the rim. With your knife, trim the edge of the dish again, thus removing all unwanted pastry and making a neat edge. Cut three slits in the centre of the pie to allow the steam to escape. Carefully glaze the top with a pastry brush and egg wash. Let this glazed top dry for 20 minutes. Pre-heat the oven to 180°C. Once the glazing has dried somewhat you can slide it into the middle of the pre-heated oven and cook for 25-30 minutes. It will be golden and smell amazing. When it is done, take it out of the oven with oven gloves and lay on a tea towel for at least 30 minutes before even thinking about a taste. I leave it for longer and eat it at room temperature.

Be careful not to burn your tongue, as the filling has a reputation to be of lava heat!

This pie is easy, although at first reading you may think it is complicated. You will realise that making a pie is a cool investment of time. I hope you enjoy this special time and I hope you will turn to the other pies in the book with interest.

CHEDDAR RISOTTO MILANESE (V)

SERVES 6 AS A STARTER OR 4 AS A MAIN

Milanese risotto is the pride of Milan. A lesson in balance and flavour only available to the most practised risotto chef. A lesson in balance, yes, most definitely, but this risotto is more than possible for the home chef. I am very practised at fine risotto with nearly 40 years' experience, and know a thing or two about this fine dish. Here I am unveiling a Cheddar Risotto Milanese, using the finest Cheddar to achieve the creamiest version, purely because of the Cheddar. When the cheese melts it has a creamier consistency than Parmesan or Pecorino – it just does. The depth of flavour is beautifully balanced too, bringing a more distinguished flavour. I use Arborio rice – and believe me, I have tried them all – but Arborio has the ability to cream and is kinder to the cook, hence it is perfecto for this dish. If you can, try the bone marrow on top to take the dish into the world of the restaurant.

EQUIPMENT:

2 heavy-bottomed pans –
    1 for stock, 1 for risotto
Scales
2 nice plates
Ladle
Wooden spoon

INGREDIENTS:

½ onion – finely chopped
½ stick of celery – finely chopped
1 layer of fennel – finely chopped
2 cloves garlic – very finely chopped
10g butter
1 tbsp olive oil
200g Arborio risotto rice
1 good dash of dry vermouth
2 pints of good homemade stock
Good pinch of saffron fronds
70g vintage Cheddar
1 tbsp double cream – optional at the end
Salt and white pepper
1 portion per person of beef marrow –
    optional
20cm piece of beef bone – lightly roasted
    (130°C) for 10–13 mins will release the
    marrow.

METHOD:

Firstly, set the pan of stock on heat to bring to the boil.

Put the other pan on the heat to warm the olive oil and butter. Once melted and warmed, throw in the vegetables and garlic and mix thoroughly with the oils. Put the lid on and keep the heat lowish to soften the vegetables for 4 minutes – we don't want to colour them. Take off the lid and throw in the rice, mixing the rice through with the wooden spoon to coat every piece of rice thoroughly – 1 minute. Add the good dash of dry vermouth and sizzle that into the rice for a minute, to let it absorb and cook off the alcohol. Add a ladleful of the boiling stock and start the process of stirring – on the edge of boiling – just under is my tip. This stirring will take up to 20 minutes, with a wooden spoon. My tip here is to circle the spoon anti-clockwise in the centre for 20 swirls, followed by four larger swirls from 12 o'clock to 6 o'clock in both directions on the outside. Then back to the middle and repeat. This releases the creaminess of the rice.

Add the saffron fronds and continue the swirling, topping up the risotto with stock as and when needed. Just keep it on the wetter side rather than the dry side. After 10 minutes of swirling and topping up, add the grated Cheddar and swirl it through – it will melt more or less immediately. The risotto will start taking on a creaminess from here. Add double cream here – if needed. Keep adding and swirling until 20 minutes is up and you have a lovely, bright yellow, creamy looking risotto. Season with salt and white pepper.

Serve on your nice plates with the ladle, taking care to keep it in the middle of the plate and very neat. Top with the prepared beef marrow and serve.

Buon Appetito!

CHEDDAR SOUFFLÉ (V)

SERVES 4

The famous cheese soufflé has had quite a life, from its beginnings in France during the 18th century, devised by chef Vincent La Chapelle for Madame Pompadour, mistress of Louis XV; through to the restaurants of the bourgeoisie during the 20th century. A decline in popularity throughout the Sixties and the emergence of the simpler version of the restaurant led to a falling in standards and the craft of soufflé-making became less attractive to the 'new world' chef. I guess the soufflé has had to suffer the perils of fashion and social standing as much as any other historic dish. The fashion spotlight is returning in the 21st century and the cheese soufflé is returning to the fine-dining restaurant. Very much a highlight in London on the à la carte starter menu, receiving well-deserved plaudits from the culinary press, who are now 'loved up' with the art of soufflé-making and the art of serving the said 'puff' of air. Tuxedoed waiters with an air of proud professionalism are the preferred vehicle for the hot soufflé direct from the kitchen, thus applying the required clarity of this (now) most respected beginning of a special fine-dining experience. All this is available to the keen home cook and here I have a well-honed recipe for you to impress friends with. All that is needed for the home chef is good, high soufflé ramekins, good eggs and a fine, sharp Cheddar of some distinction; preferably from Somerset. The stages of construction are actually not so difficult if followed very closely. I would accompany this soufflé with a glass of fine Burgundy red or a coupe de Champagne; both are perfect partners for my Cheddar soufflé.

EQUIPMENT:

4 high-sided soufflé ramekins

Heavy-bottomed pan for the béchamel

Hand whisk for the béchamel

Electric whisk for the egg whites

Wooden spoon

Grater

Roasting tray to hold the ramekins and boiling water

Oven gloves

INGREDIENTS:

4 fresh eggs – separated

50g good butter – plus more to grease ramekins

A few gratings of Parmesan for dusting the ramekins

40g plain flour

Whole milk – approx. 125ml

Good shake of mustard powder – to your taste

120g vintage Cheddar

Salt and white pepper

METHOD:

Grease your ramekins with butter and grate the parmesan into each ramekin to coat the inside – set aside.

Set the oven to 180°C.

Make your béchamel. In the pan, melt the butter on a medium heat. Add the flour and combine with the wooden spoon – making a roux. 'Toast' the roux in the pan, by turning down the heat and 'cooking out' whilst still turning it through with the wooden spoon for a minute. Add the milk slowly, whilst hand-whisking to make a smooth sauce – you are looking for a thick and smooth, shiny sauce here; not too thick though and certainly not too slack. More whisking at this point helps make a good smooth sauce. Add the mustard powder, Cheddar and continue whisking to aid the melting of the cheese. Take off the heat and allow the ingredients to sit for a minute before adding 3 egg yolks and combining well. Season with salt and white pepper. Don't be shy of over seasoning here, as this mix will be essentially diluted by the egg whites.

Whisk the egg whites to stiff peaks, but not too stiff.

Incorporate a quarter of the egg white into the cooled béchamel and thoroughly combine.

With a palette knife or a large spoon, we need to fold the remaining egg white into the cooled béchamel. Your aim here is to just slow down your movements and to 'figure-of-eight' your motions to just about combine the egg white with the sauce.

Boil a full kettle of water. Have your roasting tray ready to take the filled ramekins. Spoon the soufflé into each ramekin, being careful not to disturb the air bubbles. Bring the mix to the top of the ramekin – take a 'slice' off the top, by sliding over the palette knife, thus flattening the soufflé at the top. Place the ramekin in the roasting tray. Repeat with the other 3 ramekins.

Take the roasting tray over to the preheated oven and slide the oven shelf out to take the roasting tray. Only now should you half fill the roasting tray with the boiling water to halfway up the ramekins, before sliding all into the middle of the oven for 18 minutes.

Carefully take the hot roasting tray from the oven and quickly serve up to your guests – who have poured you a lovely glass of well-deserved liquor to accompany your great Cheddar soufflés.

CHEDDAR FISHCAKES

SERVES 4

Fishcakes are one of those meals that are just so much better cooked at home; they just are. Hot out of the oil and at their finest, accompanied by a salsa verde and homemade tartare sauce, what could be finer? It's going to be difficult for any restaurant to match what you can achieve at home. Then we just have to make a show of the ingredients, with good solid white fish and the pink of the salmon, whipped up with mashed potato and puy lentils. I've made additions of cockles and crayfish tails, but the fishmonger had them in and I used them. The beauty of this kind of recipe is that we don't stick to it perfectly, but we utilise what the fishmonger has and what we can afford. A freshly cooked fishcake made well is great as long as you keep loosely to this recipe. Bon appétit.

EQUIPMENT:

Heavy-based pan, large enough for deep frying

Potato ricer (Google it if you're not sure what they are)

Roasting tray

Slotted spoon

Kitchen foil

Mixing bowl

Wooden spoon

3 dessert bowls for the flour, egg, breadcrumbs

Kitchen roll

Jug

Sieve

INGREDIENTS:

150g salmon or smoked haddock

150g good fresh white fish

30g cockles

30g crayfish tails

800ml whole milk

2 tbsp peas

1 tbsp capers

20 capers for tartare sauce

2 tbsp puy lentils

Garlic clove

½ fennel – chopped

2 sticks celery – chopped

Handful of parsley – chopped

40g butter & 30g flour – for roux

1 tsp English mustard

80-100g sharp Cheddar – grated

4-5 King Edward potatoes – peeled and chopped for boiling

In the 3 dessert bowls: 3 tbsp plain flour, 2 eggs beaten, 3 tbsp breadcrumbs

1 ltr sunflower oil – for deep frying

2 tbsp mayo

3 gherkins – chopped

Salt and white pepper

METHOD:

We need to poach the fish first in the roasting tray, which will cook on top of the hob. Add the milk and the chopped celery, fennel and parsley. Add all the fish and shellfish. Cook very gently for 5 minutes. Turn off the heat and allow the fish to sit in the milk for 5 minutes. Take out the fish and sieve the milk into a jug.

Boil the peeled potatoes until tender and then drain. In a bowl big enough to take the mash, put the potatoes through the potato ricer. Add some of the poaching milk and a dollop of butter and the mustard. Mix through and you have a smooth mashed potato. Set aside.

In a large mixing bowl, throw in the mash, fish, cockles, crayfish, capers, puy lentils, peas, cheese and mix with your fingers. Taste and decide on seasoning. The cheese taste should be nice and noticeable too.

Prepare your 3 dessert bowls of plain flour, 2 split and beaten eggs, and breadcrumbs (either shop-bought or whizzed from stale bread). Have a bowl of water at hand and a towel.

Bring your sunflower oil up to heat. When you can see a piece of bread sizzling in the oil it is ready to fry. Be careful here, but just throw in a little rip of bread and keep your eye on it.

When ready, take a handful of fish/potato mix and round it in your wet hands. Roll it in the flour to coat completely, then roll in the beaten eggs, and then roll in the breadcrumbs.

Then, once more, roll in the eggs and then the breadcrumbs. This is quite a faff and takes some getting used to so don't feel inadequate, just persevere.

Offer up the fishcake to the hot oil. Turn down the oil to a heat that helps it maintain its heat and not overheat. Fry the fishcakes until golden and fishcake-smelling. Lovely.

Salsa Verde:

This is easy to throw together if you have a mortar and pestle.

Throw in a garlic clove and a pinch of salt. Pulp these in the mortar. Add a grasp of parsley and pulp again. Add 20 capers and pulp again. Add olive oil and start using a spoon to mix. Add lemon juice and pepper. You now have a salsa verde.

Tartare Sauce:

Take 2 tbsp of mayo and add 20 capers, chopped gherkins and parsley. Mix and you have a tartare sauce. Easy.

You'll enjoy this dish and come back to it again and again.

CRAB AND CHEDDAR SOUFFLÉS

SERVES 4

Anybody who has experienced a crab sandwich on brown bread, cut in triangles, served with English tea and accompanied with lashings of sunshine and a clear view of the harbour and marine traffic, will understand the reason for this recipe. There are many takes on the cheese soufflé and I have tried a lot of them. If I were pushed to choose my favourite addition to fine Cheddar, it would have to be lovely, creamy and fresh crab. Crab and Cheddar are wonderful bedfellows and beautifully English. The beauty of this recipe is that you can use the exact same recipe for Cheddar soufflés, but at stage 5 you incorporate the already prepared crab as required

INGREDIENTS: before adding to stage 5 of Cheddar soufflé

2 dressed crabs – or 1 and a bit, depending on size

Fresh dill – to suit your taste

Pinch of chilli flakes – to suit your taste

Dash of nam pla (Thai fish sauce) – optional

Squeeze of lemon juice

Salt and white pepper – don't be afraid to over-season, as it will be diluted
  by the egg whites

METHOD:

In a bowl, mix all of the above until it goes nice and creamy and pink. Set aside for stage 5 of Cheddar soufflé. Add with confidence and proceed as directed.

Enjoy that little bit of Englishness with quiet contemplation.

COD FILLET GRATIN SHARER

SERVES 2

The French are the greatest exponents of a good gratin, which utilises all the cheap ingredients, mixed together with care and piled onto a fish fillet to be baked to perfection. Crispy and savoury with a citric edge is the coat a good cod fillet deserves, dabbed with little knobs of butter, helping the gratin to brown. The gratin also protects the fresh and meaty cod from overcooking and therefore points toward the wonderful French cuisine, developed with both care and frugality in mind. The word gratin comes from French word 'gratter', meaning to scrape or grate – either bread or cheese and I have decided to use both of these ingredients with a little help from some lime zest, capers and a good olive oil. The art here is to 'lift and drop' the mixture as you add to it – allowing the mix to fall through your fingers as it drops is the key to a good gratin – thus keeping it light and separated. A good seasoning and you're ready to step into a new world of fish cookery. Twinned with fresh clams, cooked in cider, onion and garlic is the perfect way to bring a great sharer to the table for a date night or just a night in together.

Quick, simple and special.

EQUIPMENT:

Bowl to take the gratin

Baking sheet or Swiss roll baking tray

Grater

Liquidiser

Zester

Large pan to cook the clams – if using

Large plate to take the sharer with ease

Wide spatula for lifting the gratin once cooked

INGREDIENTS:

15g sourdough or similar bread for topping

Large chunky fillet piece of cod from a bigger fish – 300g will suffice – skin on

A little butter for greasing and dabbing the gratin

70g sharp Cheddar – grated

500ml cider

1 tsp of capers

Zest of 1 lime

Pinch of chilli flakes

Salt and freshly ground black pepper

1lb fresh clams – frozen will do at a pinch

½ shallot – finely diced

2 cloves garlic – finely diced

Parsley – finely chopped

Dash of single cream

METHOD:

Set oven at 180°C.

Take 15g of stale sourdough bread (or similar) and throw in the liquidiser to make your breadcrumbs. I like them fine, but it's completely up to you how fine you make them. Pour them into your mixing bowl and then grate over the Cheddar. Lightly 'lift and drop' the mixture to combine lightly, add the capers and repeat. Add the lime zest – amount to suit you – and lift and drop it through. Add 1–2 tbsp good olive oil and lift and drop it through. Think about seasoning now to refine the taste.

At this point you can cook the clams in your big pan. Keep the pan ready for when the fish is 10 minutes from finished.

Clams:

First, add the finely diced shallot into the warmed olive oil, 2 cloves of garlic to soften, then an opened net of clams, and finally up to 500ml of cider. Bring to the boil and simmer with lid on for 5 minutes, until the clams are all open. Add some chopped parsley and a dash of single cream and they're ready.

Fish:

Wash the fish and pat dry. Place in the middle of a greased baking tray. Take a good handful of gratin and sit it on top of the fillet, pressing down lightly to just 'lock' it in place. Take the rest of the gratin and fashion it over and around the fillet to fully cover it. Dab on 6 little knobs of butter and slide into the middle of your oven for 22 minutes. The gratin should be beautifully browned and smell savoury once retrieved from the oven.

Serving:

Carefully lift the gratin off the baking tray and set in the middle of your large plate. Surround with the piping hot clams and a light pinch of chilli flakes – you're ready to share a great dish with your significant other.

Bon Appetit.

(NEARLY) TRADITIONAL TORTILLA ESPANOLA (V)

SERVES 6–8 DEPENDING ON APPETITE

A perfectly cooked tortilla is something to behold and is one of my desert island dishes, if pushed – the savoury exterior tickling the appetite button with umami, smugly concealing the perfectly soft and giving potatoes and sweet onions. For me it is a match made in culinary heaven. Here I have played with tradition and added some extra umami character to this Spanish delight. There is definitely a savoury boost from the aged vintage Cheddar, just deep enough to discern. As we are attempting to improve tradition, I thought I would doff my cap to the astounding Spanish pimenton/paprika ingredient – dry smoked in their tonnes in middle Spain by multi-generational paprika manufacturers. I used the sweet smoked paprika for this dish to match the sweet onion. The addition of the grated Cheddar was a no-brainer for me, entering the recipe at just the right point and thus appreciating the stages of tradition. For me the tortilla has come home with these supplementary flavours. Bringing the balance of creamy smokiness was my intention and I hope you appreciate my efforts here.

The enjoyment of traditionally turning the potato/onion mix is not lost here. It was the tradition of cooking the tortilla that attracted me to it in the first place. Touching culinary tradition is one of my favourite pastimes. Give it a go and feel the warmth of the Spanish sunshine.

Eat a tortilla at room temperature every time – not from the fridge.

EQUIPMENT:

24cm non-stick frying pan

An implement for turning the potatoes without breaking them up too much

Mixing bowl

Hand whisk

Plate that fits on top of the frying pan snugly – not too shiny

INGREDIENTS:

125ml great olive oil – it will pay in dividends

1 medium onion – roughly chopped

3 medium Maris Piper potatoes – peeled and quartered, then cut into 4mm slices

6 medium eggs

Good pinch of sweet smoked paprika

60g sharp vintage Cheddar – grated

Pinch of salt

A good few grinds of black pepper

METHOD:

Take your frying pan, add the olive oil and bring up to a medium heat. Fry the onion for 5–6 minutes until translucent and nearly a little crispy on the edge. Add the potatoes and cook for a further 2 minutes. Turn them over now with a wooden spoon. Cook the potatoes until softened, maybe with a lid, and turn carefully for 22 minutes.

When the potato gives to the bite, give the eggs and paprika a whisk in a bowl, but don't whisk too much. Add the grated Cheddar, salt and freshly ground black pepper. Take the potatoes off the heat and slide them into the bowl with the eggs, Cheddar and paprika. Give them a good mix over the potatoes.

Pour this mixture back into the pan and start cooking again on a low medium heat. Cook for 4 minutes on medium heat and then turn down a little and cover the pan for another 5 minutes or so.

I have a plate that fits snugly on top of my frying pan and this makes the next step a little easier. Put the plate on top of the frying pan and turn the whole pan and plate straight over until it is completely inverted. Then slide the upturned tortilla back in the frying pan to finish cooking.

You are looking for the egg to be just cooked in the middle, but cooked enough to bring all the ingredients together.

NB: If you don't fancy the upturning, you could finish the dish under the grill which works just as well.

"Hemingway took a large slurp of his wine, wiped his chin roughly and made it his job to devour his Spanish tortilla."

Enjoy like Hemingway.

CRUNCHY 'SMASH' BACON AND CHEESE BAGUETTE

SERVES 2

Breakfast starts the day, but what kind of day are you planning? If you're feeling indulgent and want to smash breakfast out of sight then this crunchy baguette could be up your street (as it were). Maybe it's a weekend day or maybe it's a smash sandwich for supper, just follow your nose on this one. Fresh baguette is good, but a day-old one works just as well; toasted and topped with grilled cheese, it will hide any freshness queries. I cook the bacon between two baking sheets in the oven, keeping it flat and crunchy too. A quick 2-egg mushroom omelette tops up this leviathan, flanked by smokey BBQ sauce and aioli … Ooosh.

EQUIPMENT:

3 baking sheets

Non-stick frying pan

Good reliable spatula
– for the omelette

INGREDIENTS:

Baguette – I make my own

Smoked streaky bacon – 6 slices

100g fine vintage Cheddar – grated or sliced

2 eggs

3 mushrooms – sliced

Knob of butter

Dash of sunflower oil

Smokey BBQ sauce and aioli

Fresh organic rocket – better flavour

Freshly ground pepper

METHOD:

Set the oven to 180°C.

Lay a baking sheet upside down and lay your 6 slices of streaky bacon on there. Put another baking sheet on top the right way up, so the two flat sides are touching. Slide this into the oven for 12 minutes or so – just keep peaking, by lifting the top baking sheet and putting back. Once cooked and crispy and deep-coloured, set aside.

Put the grill on full.

Halve the baguette for the two of you – one half each.

Halve each portion down the middle to then butterfly it ready for toasting. Slide them onto a baking sheet flat side down and toast a good colour into the baguette. Once toasted, grate over the Cheddar to cover the flat side and slide back on the baking sheet and under the hot grill. Grill the cheese until just perfect. Remove from the grill.

In the frying pan, drop in the knob of butter and dash of oil, heat up and cook out the mushrooms. Season at this point. Crack the two eggs directly into the pan and swirl generously with the end of the wooden spoon to distribute the egg fully. Turn down the heat. When done, flip it over to create a half moon and set aside.

You're now ready to assemble the baguette.

Spoon over a tsp each of BBQ sauce and aioli onto the grilled cheese. Top with 3 slices of the crispy bacon, then top this with half of the small omelette. Throw on some rocket and lots of pepper.

For stability, use a knife through the middle to keep it all together.

You can now smash it over the net for an ace!

IL BARATTOLO DELLA LIBERTA (V)

SERVES 2

'The tin of freedom', where the cook can open his or her wings and fly solo, using the basics to start and then discovering the art of ingredient freedom, to pitch the dish just where you want it to go. I find that exercising this initiative always pays dividends. I see flavours as an artist sees colours and cooking this way exercises that creative side of the brain. My version has a reduced, creamy and cheesy pasta sauce, layered with fresh kale and ripped chunks of stale sourdough bread, baked on top of fresh thyme and garlic and drizzled with olive oil – creating a crunchy Italian feel and very much reminding me of trips to Sorrento and the Amalfi Coast. I have added my Cheddar crispy 'disc – used in the ice cream to push the umami button – and voila, we have a dish coming together. So, all bases are covered and we just need to make it a home run. I decided to use the attractive Italian tomato tin to cradle this dish and to serve it at the table just so. My thinking being, that this could be the catalyst to making that home run and it works really well. Cooking that takes a further leap off the plate and shows a creative edge is always a cool angle at the table, I find.

It's fun to raid the fridge/larder for the aging ingredients and meld them into something special, as well as being good food management in the kitchen. Keeping food waste to a minimum is one of my standard considerations now and is relatively easy to achieve if you can muster up a dish like this occasionally.

My Version ...

EQUIPMENT:

Equipment:

2 empty tins of Italian tomatoes

2 heavy-based pans

Roasting tin – for the bread

24cm non-stick frying pan

Kitchen roll

Plastic spatula

INGREDIENTS:

1 tbsp olive oil

½ onion – chopped

1 clove of garlic – chopped

½ parsnip – peeled and chopped

Handful of kale

Ripped quarter of a loaf – a rustic loaf is perfect

Fresh thyme leaves – stripped from the sprig

50ml chicken stock

2 tins of plum tomatoes

Dash of balsamic vinegar

Dash of white wine

10g mushrooms – chopped

60ml double cream

25g aged Cheddar – grated

20g Parmesan – grated

30g pasta – any you have in

Handful of basil to garnish

Parsley to garnish

METHOD:

Heat the olive oil in the pan and add the onion, thyme and parsley. Give a swirl and cook on low with the lid on for 5 minutes. Turn up the heat a bit. Add the stock and swirl. Add the tomatoes, parsnip and mushrooms and allow to heat through before breaking the tomatoes up. Add the balsamic vinegar and wine, swirl and cook out for a minute. Add the double cream, swirl. Add the Cheddar and Parmesan and watch them melt. Add the chosen pasta. Swirl and taste to assess the required seasoning. Turn down to simmer for 10 minutes to cover the time for the pasta to cook and give the creaminess time to develop. Set aside.

In a medium pan, boil the kale for 10 minutes and set aside.

In a preheated oven at 180°C, bake the bread on top of the thyme and garlic, drizzled with olive oil, for 15 minutes to give a garlicky crunch. Set aside.

In your reserved tins we will now build the dish: a layer of pasta sauce, followed by a layer of vibrant green kale, and a chunk or two of crispy bread. Repeat to the top of the tin. Try to make the sauce come to the top too. You may need a little more stock to mix into the sauce to help that.

Put in the oven for 25 minutes to cook through and allow the sauce to stick to the sides of the tin.

In the meantime, cook the grated Cheddar in your dry frying pan on a medium-hot hob, by dropping into the middle of the pan and allowing it to melt. Once melted and giving up its oils, turn down a tad and wait for it to take on a great aroma and a bronze appearance – it will begin to smoke, but this is good. Take off the hob and lay the pan on something cool to hasten the cooling. After a minute take a plastic spatula and lift the edge of your cheese disc. It should just come away and now you can place it on the kitchen roll to crispen up. Set aside.

Carefully take the pasta dish from the oven and allow to cool considerably, as it will be as hot as lava. Dress with some fresh basil and half of your cheese disc each.

Bella, bella!

CHEDDAR PAN HAGGERTY (V)

SERVES 8

The enigma that is pan haggerty. An enigma because it has very little written history or records before 1936 but, this dish has been a common meal in Northumberland, enough to give it a nickname. Historians suspect this was a Victorian working-class dish that travelled with housewives for quite a number of years. There was very little written education within these hard working classes but it was recorded in *The Episode of the Pan Haggerty* by F.E. Doran in the BBC Northern Services production of the same name in 1936. A simple collection of potatoes and onions with an option of adding ham or corned beef, according to the original recipe. Simply slice the vegetables thinly and layer in a frying pan. The original has a turnover/inversion of the pan ingredients to colour the top, but we have a trick up our sleeve with this one. The picture shows just how beautiful this dish can be and the savoury aroma is quite spectacular from the addition of vintage Cheddar.

EQUIPMENT:

24cm frying pan

3 bowls to hold vegetables and cheese

Grater

Plastic spatula

Mandolin/slicer or a sharp knife

Plate larger than the frying pan – or wooden cutting board

INGREDIENTS:

1 tbsp groundnut oil

10g butter

Plus more butter for 'blobbing'

4–5 potatoes – medium-sized, unpeeled, and thinly sliced

2 medium onions – thinly sliced

200g vintage Cheddar – grated

Salt and white pepper

Sprig of thyme

METHOD:

In your frying pan warm up the oil and butter – to melt only. Bring the pan over to the work surface and set a layer of potato and a layer of onion. Add a few blobs of butter and lightly salt, but be heavier with the pepper. Top with Cheddar and continue with the layers in the following way:

Potato, onion, butter, salt, pepper, cheese, until the frying pan is full.

Back over to the hob and sit the pan on a medium heat for up to 10 minutes. We are trying to colour the bottom to a deep bronze, so 10 minutes is needed.

Set into the middle of your preheated oven for up to 45 minutes – the homely smell and appearance on top will guide you. Carefully take out with oven gloves and allow to cool slightly. Try to loosen the underside with a plastic spatula.

Place a plate or wooden cutting board over the top and carefully invert.

The pan haggerty should be revealed when you remove the inverted frying pan.

Top with a sprig of fresh thyme.

And howay ya garn.

GLASTONBURY TOR(MENTS)

SERVES 2

This one is a celebration of Somerset and their two outstanding nation's favourites: cave-aged, sharp-tasting Cheddar and beautifully fragrant, appley and alcoholic cider. This is typically cooked in a cup that contains our national stars, but also chicken breast and tarragon, another match in culinary heaven. Then all this is smoothed off with leeks and velouté sauce and topped with crispy puff pastry. The 'torment' here is not to eat them too quickly after they leave the oven, all bubbling and baked to perfection. You do have to leave this 'torment' for about 10 minutes before tackling these mothers of Somerset invention.

EQUIPMENT:

All 3 sizes of heavy-based
  pans are needed here

Sieve

Measuring jug

Whisk

Wooden spoon

2 thick cups – these are
  going to be baked, so
  good robust cups here

Egg wash brush

INGREDIENTS:

1 good chicken breast

Bunch of herbs – rosemary, thyme

Fresh tarragon for the velouté

1 leek – thinly sliced

Knob of butter for leeks

30g butter for velouté

1 tbsp plain flour

1 level tsp dry mustard

50ml good cider

100g vintage Cheddar – grated

Salt and white pepper

Chunk of shop-bought puff pastry

Egg – beaten for egg wash

METHOD:

In your medium pan, pour in enough water to just cover the whole chicken breast. Add the rosemary and thyme and poach the breast on a very low heat for 20 minutes. Once cooked remove from the water and set aside, reserving the poaching liquid.

In your large pan, melt the knob of butter before adding the leeks. Once sizzling nicely, turn down heat and put lid on and cook for about 10 minutes to soften them – they will cook down to a smallish amount.

In the small pan, melt the 30g of butter and add the flour, give it a good mix with the wooden spoon to combine – making a roux. Cook this out for one minute, but don't colour – so a medium/low heat. With a whisk to hand and a sieve, add 100ml of poaching liquid into the roux whilst whisking. Let this be absorbed by the roux and then continue – whisking all the time – by adding another 100ml of poaching liquid. Your final 100ml will go in now and you should whisk all this into a nice, smooth velouté. Add the fresh tarragon, cider and mustard to flavour the velouté. Then add the grated Cheddar and give it a good mix until smooth and tasty – this will need some seasoning. Set aside with the chicken breast.

Cut the chicken into chunks and throw into the bottom of each cup. Spoon some leeks on top of the chicken, until you get 2cm below the rim of the cup. Pour in the velouté and tap the cup to allow it to work its way down. Let the velouté stop 2cm from the rim. Sprinkle with tarragon and set aside, covered.

For the puff pastry, take it from the packaging and roll out on a lightly floured work surface to about a centimetre thick. Cut out a square bigger than the top of the cup and press onto the rim of the cup to leave an indent of its shape. Then cut around this to create a top that fits the cup perfectly. Uncover the cups and lightly butter the edge, down to the velouté. Push the pastry into the cup and down to the velouté. Egg-wash the pastry and repeat with the next cup.

Cook in a pre-heated oven at 180°C for 25 minutes or until beautifully golden and the velouté has volcanoed from the rim.

Cool these now for 10 minutes before tasting.

This is the torment!

SALT-CRUST BEETROOT (V)

MAKES 2

For me, accompaniments to cheese are a subject in themselves, but the offerings from supermarkets are lifeless at best and not the least bit imaginative. There are myriad things we can do to enhance the cheeseboard and this is one such little beauty. A salt crust surrounding a fresh beetroot, giving up the flavours of orange zest and mustard, make this dish a little special and great to serve up to friends with a creamy and ripe Camembert or a fine Somerset clothbound Cheddar. We are essentially making a quick dough and flavouring it quite heavily, to bring those flavours to the party. They transport across in a really well balanced way and the earthiness of fresh beetroot shines a little brighter because of it. No vinegar is added here, although a teaspoon of gloopy 10-year-old balsamic wouldn't go amiss. But please, no other vinegar is needed. Just sit back and watch your friends dive into something a little off the beaten track, but don't sit back too much – it will go!

EQUIPMENT:

Mixing bowl

Electric hand whisk

Rolling pin

Baking tray

Wooden spoon

Scales

Zester

INGREDIENTS:

2 fresh beetroots

130g plain flour

2 x 25g of coarse salt and fine salt – the better
the salt, the better the dish

4 sprigs fresh rosemary – finely chopped

1 heaped tsp powdered mustard

Zest of 1 orange

Whites of 2 eggs

2 tbsp cider

METHOD:

Bring all the weighed and dry ingredients together in your mixing bowl. Whip up
the egg whites with your electric hand whisk and add to the bowl. Mix carefully to
combine. Add 2 tbsp of cider to help bind the dough together. Use more cider if
needed. You are looking for a dough not too dry, but if anything just a little sticky.

Wrap in cling wrap or similar and refrigerate for 2 hours.

Top and tail, wash and drain the beetroot.

After 2 hours, set the oven to 160°C.

Unwrap the dough and split into 2 equal pieces. On a lightly floured work surface,
roll out one of the pieces of dough to about 4mm thickness. Place a beetroot in the
centre – upside down. Bring all sides up and around the 'top' of the crust and secure,
so there are no holes showing – use some of the other dough if a hole shows, to shore
it up.

Repeat with the second piece of dough and place on a baking tray.

Cook in the middle of your preheated oven for 1½ hours.

Take from the oven and allow to cool for 10 minutes.

Take to the table with the cheeseboard and elect a guest to smash open the salt crust
with a rolling pin – it gives fairly easily, but is a good gimmick.

Dig in and enjoy.

DINNER

OUTDOOR STEAKS WITH CHEDDAR AND BREADCRUMB CRUST

SERVES 2

The art of a great steak is a multi-fold endeavour that needs some direct action before there is any success. 1: To understand the cut of meat and how the butcher can best nurture a genuinely great, aged cut. 2: To understand the outdoor cooking method. Bringing these two facets together is stage one and needs to be done well before you continue to pursue a great outdoor steak.

Here we are choosing the finest conditioned steaks from our dedicated butcher, but we are cooking them outside on a fire pit and griddle stand, covering the steaks with a breadcrumb and Cheddar coat that will then crispen and deliver the finest steak known to mankind! So, there are a number of provisos that we will need to hit before this is possible. To cook over hard wood, prepared over an hour's pre-burning and thus creating a fire ready for steaks; a griddle stand; and keeping the pan about 3–4 inches from the pan, so it is not too fierce. When all this is in place you will have to be patient and be prepared to sit on your hands; do not touch the steaks in any way for 5 minutes before you turn them – not even a prod or poke, just sit and wait and let the crust and meat develop.

The steaks I am using are not the same. I want to demonstrate two fabulous cuts to help you at the butchers. We have a rib-eye, but a cut that is as deep as the width of 2 fingers, and a new steak for you carnivores: a 'short steak', which is essentially a sirloin but with the bone still attached. They are best from a butcher that hangs their steaks for 30 days or so, and this is the kind of class of meat we are looking for.

Once you are prepared, this is the checklist that will easily help you to put these awesome steaks on a plate:

1: Great steaks at room temperature. 2: Good breadcrumbs and Cheddar. 3: A prepared fire pit, with hard wood. 4: A heavy-based frying pan or cast-iron griddle, to take 2 steaks. 5: To let the steaks rest before cutting.

EQUIPMENT:

Fire pit or equivalent for wood burning

Hard wood

Griddle stand – to safely position the steaks 3–4 inches above the fiercest heat

Tongs

Liquidiser or hand blitzer

Heavy-based frying pan or cast-iron griddle to take the steaks

Grater

2 roasting trays

A good spatula – able to get under the steaks without wrecking the crust

INGREDIENTS:

2 fine steaks – as described above

4 slices of sourdough bread – stale (dried outside for a couple of hours)

100g great vintage Cheddar

Rosemary

2 eggs – beaten

Salt and pepper

Sunflower oil

METHOD:

Give the steaks an hour to come up to room temperature. In the meantime, start the fire and lay your hard wood to burn heartily for an hour. Back in the kitchen, cut the stale sourdough – crust on – and liquidise fiercely until a good, fine crumb – about 45 seconds. Pour into a dry roasting tray and grate the Cheddar over. Finely dice your fresh rosemary and mix the three ingredients together well. Set aside.

Plate the steaks and lightly drizzle with sunflower oil and sprinkle with some more diced rosemary. Set aside.

Crack both eggs into a cup and beat. Set aside.

When the fire is good and set to continue, we are good to go with this awesome steak.

Pour the egg into the other roasting tray. Season the meat with a good salting. Douse the steaks in the egg and rub the breadcrumb mix all over the steaks – it will stick well. Plate the covered steaks and take them to the fire pit. Put the griddle or pan onto the griddle stand and allow to come to a high heat – drop water onto the pan and if it completely sizzles away, you are ready. Pour 2 tbsp of sunflower oil in the pan or griddle and wait for the oil to smoke a little. Carefully lay the coated steaks on the pan/griddle and step away from the steaks – for 5 minutes. Have a suitable spatula there to help you turn the crusty steaks over. Cook for 4–5 minutes, untouched again. Once you are happy the steaks are cooked, take off the griddle and take directly into the kitchen. Cover with foil and leave to stop sizzling.

Now is the time to set yourself a great accompaniment for these steaks. Once set and ready to go, cut into your crusty, juicy steaks with some pride.

The best part of this whole recipe is the tasting experience. Crunch through that savoury crust and then experience the tender bite of gorgeousness.

This is the new way to prepare an outdoor steak and we are now on the button with it – it doesn't get any better.

Enjoy!

EVERYDAY TOOR DHAL (V)

SERVES 2-4

We all love a dhal; simmered spicy, garlicky dhal. The list of staple Indian everyday dishes includes a number of dhal. This is my fusion version, developed with toor dhal, a much creamier and lesser-known pulse. It has a gloopy quality once it's cooked down and is considered very creamy without the addition of cream. This recipe works on that same creamy level with the addition of Cheddar. Adding to the creamy party, and in conjunction with fresh coriander and cumin, it finds its place firmly on my everyday 'go-to' list.

Try it with my Cheddar naan bread (see recipe on page 134) for that special touch.

EQUIPMENT:

Medium/large heavy-based pan
24cm frying pan
Grater

INGREDIENTS:

200g toor dhal (most Indian food shops have it) – or chana dhal

2 thick slices of ginger

Water to cover and the same amount again – keep topping up

½ tsp turmeric

2–3 tbsp sunflower oil

3 cloves of garlic – peeled and sliced thinly

1 tsp spice mix – garam masala for example, or your favourite, freshly ground. I use medium Sri Lankan curry powder, which is roasted before grinding – available in Asian spice shops

2 tomatoes – quartered

4 mushrooms – thickly sliced

½ tsp cumin

½ tsp fennel seeds

2 black or green cardamom

1 star anise – split

¼ cinnamon stick

4 curry leaves – optional

Lemon – to taste

Salt and pepper – to taste

60g grated Cheddar – vintage if possible

Coriander – chopped for garnish and flavour

METHOD:

In a medium-sized, heavy-based pan, pour in the toor dhal and cover with water and the extra amount, with the ginger slices and turmeric thrown in. Bring to the boil and then simmer for up to an hour. Keep stirring from time to time and topping up as you go if needed. After the hour, you will have a gloopy, creamy, silky dhal to now work on.

Take a small frying pan and add the sunflower oil. Bring up to heat and add the sliced garlic. Cook the garlic to the biscuit-smelling and golden/brown point. Immediately pour into the dhal and watch for spluttering as it comes into contact with the dhal.

Add the curry powder and mix thoroughly. Add the tomatoes and mix it all through.
Leave on a low simmer.

In the frying pan add a little oil and the sliced mushrooms. After 2 minutes add the
cumin seeds and cook out for a minute.

Slide these into the dhal and mix through again.

Add the cumin, fennel, star anise, cardamom, cinnamon and curry leaves.

Cook for 30 minutes to amalgamate the flavours.

Grate in the Cheddar and watch it melt into the mix and smell the heavenliness.

Top up with water, if needed, to make it a little gloopy – not too much though.

Finish with some chopped fresh coriander and you're ready to serve up or turn off
for later.

Just before you serve, season up with fresh lemon juice.

AUTHENTIC CHEESE NAAN BREAD ^(V)

MAKES 4 BREADS

Having cooked Indian for nearly 40 years and had the best vegetarian Indian restaurant outside London in my local town, I have been a little spoilt with authentic breads. This one I have worked on for a year or so and feel I have now perfected a good cookbook version that has a mark of authentic class about it and works every time. You can even refrigerate them overnight for great results the next day. If you love Indian breads, it's a must try.

EQUIPMENT:
Bread mixing bowl
2 baking trays
Pastry brush
Grater
Shower cap or dampened towel

INGREDIENTS:
250g warm water – yes, grams
   for accuracy
1 tsp sugar
10g dried active yeast
500g strong bread flour
1 tsp baking powder
200g vintage Cheddar
1 level tsp salt
2 tbsp natural yoghurt
For Garlic Emulsion:
15g butter/glug of olive oil
3–4 cloves garlic – chopped
Small grasp of coriander
½ tsp fresh cumin seeds

METHOD:

For this recipe you will need a large bowl for bread-making. Put the oven on 100°C or so and warm the bowl for 5 minutes. Prepare a jug of warm water and your scales (ready to measure out) the sugar and yeast. Carefully take the bowl from the oven and combine the weighed water, sugar and yeast, mix through and leave to foam up after 5 minutes. Turn off the oven, but keep closed and warm for later.

Weigh out the flour and add the salt and baking powder.

After the 5-minute wait for the bowl and the foaming mix, add the dry ingredients you have prepared. Mix them either by hand or with a KitchenAid – either way add the yoghurt after a minute of mixing. You will find that the kneading produces a smooth and slightly tacky dough after 5–7 minutes of kneading.

Shape into a smooth ball, place in the warmed bowl and cover with a dampened towel or shower cap! Yes, a shower cap works really well and helps us from overusing cling film.

Leave in the warmed oven for 1 hour to rise.

Once risen, take from the oven and empty the bowl onto a floured work surface or cutting board. Cover lightly with the flour and roughly roll the dough into a thick sausage shape, approximately 12x4 inches.

Split this dough into four equal parts and leave three portions back in the warm bowl and cover.

Take the one portion you have chosen and roughly roll with your rolling pin to a circle about 1 cm thick. No finesse is needed here, just a rough circle, but not too thin.

Grate your cheese onto a plate and take a quarter of it and place in the middle of the rolled circle of dough, leaving a 2–3cm margin of dough around the outside.

Lift up the margins of dough and shape by pulling upwards to make a sack around the cheese, pinching and pinching until it is secured and essentially (now) a ball with no openings revealing the cheese.

With the join facing you, turn over the dough so the join is now on the bottom. Lightly flour and roll again into a circle, roughly 10–12 inches.

You have now just made your first cheese naan.

You need to prepare for the second rise now.

Take the two baking sheets and lightly flour them both.

Lay your naans lightly on the baking sheets and flour the top of each naan.

Cover lightly for half an hour in a warm environment.

Prepare your garlic, coriander and cumin wash by melting the butter/oil in a non-stick frying pan on a medium heat. Colour the garlic until lightly golden and biscuit-smelling. Take off the heat now and add the chopped coriander and cumin seeds. Let them just sit, with a spoon, ready for the final moments.

Set the oven to 180°C.

Remove the light covering from the naan and throw into the hot oven for 15–18 minutes keeping an eye on the doneness. They will puff up and look very impressive. They may even burst a little and lose some cheese, but no matter, just continue cooking until they are golden and ready.

Once they look just perfect, carefully take them from the oven and spoon over your warmed garlic wash to run down the sides of your fresh and awesome naan.

Serve with an amount of culinary pride.

These breads are awesome and you should be making these for years.

CACIO E PEPE IN A CHEDDAR BASKET (V)

A famous dish in Rome, made even more famous by the focused appreciation of Anthony Bourdain in his special monochrome episode where he visited Restaurant X – so named because the owners wanted to keep their anonymity and thus not be inundated with hordes of pilgrimages of keen foodies wanting to walk in Bourdain's 'specially selected' steps. This dish is achingly simple in essence, but not so simple in real time. There are certain preparations that need to be in place to match the quick stages of construction – nothing too demanding though and the pay-off is as sexy as Bourdain promised. Sexy, because the cheese and pepper (cacio e pepe) pasta is skilfully rolled onto tongs and placed into a wisplike and super savoury Cheddar basket. The gentlest of touches will snap away some basket and, accompanied by the cheese and spicy pepper in the mouth, evokes a celestial cavalcade of cherubs and angels veritably diving out of a Caravaggio masterpiece, accompanied by a bank of royal trumpets announcing the God of Savoury Food is about to appear as a Roman apparition. Yes, cheesemeisters. It's that good and it is that savoury gorgeous that I have it on my desert island list of all-time favourites. Safe to say, it comes well recommended by the irrepressible Bourdain and by yours truly. Keep the faith and all will be repaid – and watch the episode on YouTube.

EQUIPMENT:

Large, heavy-bottomed pasta pan with lid

24cm non-stick frying pan

Mould to shape your basket – a dish with depth but not too wide

Pasta tongs – or fork and spoon

Pepper grinder

Grater

2 ramekins to split 2 eggs

Non-metal spatula

Cup for the starchy pasta water

INGREDIENTS:

60g Cheddar for each disc

Enough good spaghetti for the number of diners

15g x 2 of Pecorino Romano and Parmigiano Reggiano per diner

Freshly ground pepper

2 egg yolks

Olive oil

METHOD:

First we need to cook and prepare the Cheddar disc. Heat your dry frying pan to a good heat and grate the Cheddar straight onto the pan. Turn up the heat a little and watch the cheese melt and really begin to bubble. Let the bubble continue and then watch the fats being released – this is all to be expected – until the colour begins to change to a light tan. Turn down the heat a little and watch the colour darken to a light bronze.

Take off the heat and lay the pan on something cold – the sink top or something similar. Here we have to use our judgement well. We are looking to use a plastic spatula to peel the cheese off the pan. Too early and the cheese is still liquid; too late and the cheese is too hard. We need to find the 'sweet spot' where the pan gives up the ghost and releases the Cheddar disc easily. This is not too difficult – it just sounds it!

Once released from the pan, you will find the disc is really hot and pliable. Moving quickly, offer it up to the mould you have prepared and slowly push it into position before it cools too much and snaps.

Once in position you can set the basket aside, but not in a fridge.

Now for the pasta. Heat a pan full of water and salt it good. Once boiling add the pasta and make sure all strands are covered. Cook for 7 minutes or until it reaches your preferred doneness. Before you fully drain the pasta water – leave the hob on heat – have a cup set in the sink and fill the cup with pasta water before draining the rest away.

Place the pasta back in the pan and add 1 tbsp of good olive oil and mix. Add a couple of tbsps of the starchy water and swirl manfully to combine the ingredients. This swirling will continue now until you are done. Add the egg yolks and the 2 cheeses and swirl manfully again. Start adding your ground pepper from a pepper mill – you need quite a bit of pepper but not too much – so about 20 grinds is a good start!

You should need to add a little more starch water, allowing you to find the sweet spot of consistency – creamy and cheesy. Perfecto.

Make sure your (very fragile and crispy) Cheddar basket is placed in its final destination, on just the right plate.

Wind your cacio e pepe onto your fork or tongs and carefully offer up to the baskets, taking good care here so as not to split the basket. It's just a case of being careful, really.

Sprinkle with some cheese and a last grind of pepper and you have one hell of a sexy plate right there.

God bless Anthony Bourdain and God bless cacio e pepe.

GALICIAN FISHERMAN'S GRATIN

SERVES 4

Spanish cuisine is vibrant and exciting to me, as a cook. The splash of red from the paprika, the citrus punch of Seville orange, the pungent purple Spanish garlic, all combine to give us proud Galician tones. The use of olive oil is ubiquitous throughout Spain and heavily used. Indeed there is more olive oil produced in Spain than anywhere else in the world. Their olive oil makes a great basis for lots of their sauces and here is no exception. We are bringing two other ubiquitous Spanish ingredients: garlic (ajo) and the superbly hand-smoked (from La Mancha) paprika. I wanted to combine these flavours and plunge them straight into a coastal peasant dish of hake with peppers and garlic. Combine these flavours with Cheddar and you have a dish of instant savoury umami and creaminess; just finishing this dish with this extra (and needed) creamy Cheddar is important here. I do use Cheddar as a flavouring a lot, where I am using the flavour to enhance a dish rather than dominate – just like using a seasoning to bring out the heart of a recipe. For me, Spanish food has its heart in the people; living on the edge, this dogged and tough cuisine has the power to evoke the hard-fought past with a single bite. No wonder Hemingway chose his robust and evocative rhetoric to describe the Spanish way of life, perfectly demonstrating the Galician passion of his beloved nation – as if the heart of a Spaniard beats harder and faster, with a more edgy culture than any other. For me, Spanish food manifests this beating heart.

EQUIPMENT:
2 pans for boiling

Bowl for stock

1.5ltr Pyrex/glass casserole dish with lid

Or a 1.5ltr casserole dish of any kind

Baking sheet

INGREDIENTS:
½ red and green peppers – sliced lengthways

4 medium waxy potatoes – unpeeled and 3mm sliced

1 onion – peeled and halved

4 cloves of garlic – chopped

3 tsp smoked paprika

70-80g Cheddar – grated

1 nice thick fillet of hake – skin on

1 large tiger prawn each

Capers – to sprinkle

Salt and pepper

Olive oil

METHOD:
Firstly, fill your pans with water and throw half an onion into each pan. Bring to the boil and simmer gently. In one pan throw in the peppers, and in the other throw in the sliced potato. After 10 minutes slide the hake into the peppers pan and turn off the potato pan. After a further 5 minutes of poaching the hake, drain the hake pan into a bowl and set aside (as a stock). Pour away the potato water and set aside the potatoes.

Set oven to 180°C.

In another pan pour 5 tbsp olive oil, bring to heat and add the garlic. Cook until the kitchen is filled with garlic fumes – don't colour the garlic. Turn down the heat, add the 4 tsp paprika and stir in. Add some fish stock, about 8–10 tbsp and mix to combine. Salt well.

Now layer the casserole dish. Firstly add the potatoes, then peppers, then fish, and finally cheese. Repeat until you have 3 layers. The top layer will be potato and the three tiger prawns.

Tablespoon the sauce of paprika and garlic into the dish until it comes to ⅔ full.

Grate Cheddar on top of the dish and place onto your baking tray.

Cook in the preheated oven for 15 minutes and nicely coloured on top with a lovely cheesy gratin.

Take from the oven and let it cool a little before plating up and sprinkling with capers and freshly ground pepper.

(LA MANCHA) SPANISH GARLIC SOUP

SERVES 4

The middle of Spain, the flatlands that are either ignored or driven through on your way to the coast. La Mancha holds some Spanish jewels and one of them is the purple-hued garlic that is ubiquitous in Spain. Large vibrant bulbs with a rich, garlicky flavour, not overly strong, is the garlic that inspired my culinary juices to drive me to make a highly flavoured chicken stock – this helped me with the flavour I was picturing. This is a peasant dish which thanks the cook for the use of good stock and ingredients. Find a good smoked paprika, made from the pimento and hand-smoke-dried in large drying houses of oak wood – the only wood allowed for the use of smoking pimento – the peppers are hand layered by the farmer, with his pitchfork, for two weeks. They are then milled by electrically powered stone wheels. The three varieties are: dulce – sweet and mild; agridulce – bittersweet, medium hot: and picante – hot. The choice is yours but I tend to use a mix of dulce and agridulce. Don't be put off by the amount of garlic here, the flavour is high on the gorgeous scale and is one of our favourite treats.

EQUIPMENT:

Your favourite, heavy-
   bottomed pan for soup

Pan for chicken stock

Wooden spoon

Ladle

Sieve

Bowl

Baking tray

INGREDIENTS:

2 tbsp olive oil

1 whole bulb of vibrant-looking garlic – split
   into cloves, peeled and left whole

½ onion – chopped

5–6 good pinches of your chosen smoked
   paprika

2 pints of full flavoured chicken stock – best
   made yourself

Kettle of hot water

2 slices of crisp, crusted bread – sourdough
   for me

100g sharp Cheddar cheese – grated

Salt and freshly ground pepper

Little pinch of saffron – optional

For the Chicken Stock:

Chicken carcass, 1 stick celery, 3 halves
   onion (skin on), 1 medium carrot, a root
   vegetable like parsnip, 4 sprigs rosemary,
   4 sprigs thyme, 2 cloves garlic, paprika, 2
   bay leaves, 2 cloves

CHICKEN STOCK:

In your medium, heavy-based saucepan, fill with water to just under ⅔ full. Throw in 1–2 chicken carcasses and 3 halves of onion, 1 large carrot (unpeeled), 1 celery stalk (chopped), 2 bay leaves, 2 cloves of garlic (crushed). Bring to the boil and simmer lightly for 50 minutes. Leave to cool and sieve into a bowl.

METHOD:

In your soup pan, pour in 2 tbsp olive oil to warm through. Throw in the garlic and cook out for 5 minutes. Add the chopped onion and swirl to cook out. Add the first large pinch of paprika and mix. When the aroma smells right, add the first ladleful of chicken stock. Bring up the heat. Add another ladleful and repeat. Let the soup simmer lightly now.

Turn on the grill. Slice the bread, nice and thick. Slice the cheese and cover one side of the bread with the cheese. Lay onto a baking tray and grill – toast on one side only.

When cool enough to handle, carefully lay the bread and cheese (to float) on top of the soup. Add another ladleful of stock and the second good pinch of paprika. Sink the bread now with the ladle. You may need to use water instead of stock now, just to balance the flavour. Take a spoon and start to swirl the soup, allowing the bread to absorb some soup to then start breaking up.

Add a little more stock or water as required and a little more paprika and the little pinch of saffron, if using. Thoroughly mix and taste for salt content. Season where needed. Now it's just a question of swirling and tasting until you're happy with the soup.

The whole process will take 20 minutes from start to finish.

A truly fabulous peasant soup.

Enjoy!

LUXURY FISH PIE MAC AND CHEESE (V)

SERVES 4

Where the beloved fish pie, with all that creamy, steamy white and smoked fish meets the 21st century in a mac and cheese. Actually this dish could be called a cheese casserole and it seems that cheese casseroles date back a long way; in the 14th century it was recorded in an Italian cookbook *Liber de Coquina*, which featured a dish called Baked Parmesan Pasta. A cheese and pasta recipe was recorded in an English cookbook also in the 14th century. This book was called *Forme of Cury* and the dish was known as 'makerouns', according to Wikipedia. But I think it's fair to say that the Americans resurrected it as mac and cheese, where all kinds of ingredients are combined to create a cheese casserole, baked in the oven. This recipe is no exception, and yes, that is exactly what we are doing here, but we are going all Louisiana in the Deep South with crawfish pie ingredients of lobster, crayfish tails and cockles. You could omit the lobster if that is a bridge too far, but I have a great wet fish outlet near me and he looks after me, so lobster was a no-brainer. You need to make a bouillabaisse sauce in this recipe (with the tiger prawn shells) and I recommend you make it beforehand to save any nonsense on the day.

EQUIPMENT:
Medium heavy-based pan for bouillabaisse sauce
Rolling pin – to smash the shells
Lighter for flambé – if working on electric

Pan for boiling macaroni
Large pan with lid for lobster
Sieve and bowl for sauce
Casserole dish to serve 4 – usually 1.5ltr
Lobster crackers
24cm frying pan

INGREDIENTS:
Bouillabaisse Sauce:
(Makes 250ml)
10 shell-on raw tiger prawns
½ onion – chopped
3 cloves of garlic – chopped
150ml cider
150ml tomato passata
Fresh thyme leaves
Brandy to flambé – a dash
Dash of Pernod
Fennel seeds
Fresh orange juice – squeezed from the fruit
Pinch of saffron – optional
Cider – to deglaze
Up to 100ml single cream – it's up to you really
Salt and pepper

On the Day:
1 live lobster or frozen from supermarket
150g macaroni
Olive oil
2 garlic cloves – smashed with the back of a knife
24 x 100g fresh hake – skin on
10 raw prawns – already peeled from sauce
100g crawfish tails
80g cockles
Jar of peppers
130g fresh or frozen peas
250ml bouillabaisse sauce – already made
100g sharp Cheddar – grated

142

METHOD:

Bouillabaisse Sauce:

In your pan, warm the olive oil and add the thyme leaves, onion and garlic. Cook out to soften and become fragrant. Throw in the peeled skins of the prawns and turn up the heat. Swirl them through and smash the shells with your rolling pin to extract all the goodness, for 3–4 minutes. Throw on a dash of brandy and light the alcohol into a flambé – be careful here not to go mad, as a lot of cooker hoods are greasy and they can catch alight, so be careful. Let the flambé die down and add the tomato passata, fennel seeds and Pernod. Swirl them through to combine and cook them on high to entice the flavour out of the shells. Turn down the heat a little now. Add the cider and orange juice and start to reduce the sauce. You may need to de-scum the top with a tablespoon to keep the sauce clean of impurities. You can add a pinch of saffron at this point, but that's optional. Reduce it down until you are happy with the flavour. Add single cream and reduce for another 10 minutes. Sieve the sauce into a bowl and season carefully. Set aside. You can use this sauce for pasta with crab or scallops, etc. – it's a great seafood 'go-to' sauce.

On the Day:

Boil up the macaroni until cooked. Drain and set aside. Kill the lobster quickly and humanely by plunging your sharp knife into the centre of the cross that naturally occurs on the top of the head. Cook your Lobster in the large pan in lots of salty water for 15 minutes. Drain and cover with cold water to stop the cooking process. Crack off the tail and open the underside with scissors to reveal the white lobster tail flesh. Crack the claws with lobster crackers (like Brazil nut crackers). Keep the shells to make another bouillabaisse sauce to freeze. Prepare your fish by seasoning well, ready for stacking the casserole. Have your sauce ready and waiting, with your macaroni and raw prawns.

In a 24cm frying pan add olive oil and 2 smashed cloves of garlic, bring up to heat and cook the seasoned fish skin side down for 2 minutes on high. Turn over and briefly cook the underside. Set aside. You want to undercook the fish because it will continue cooking in the oven. Deglaze the pan with cider and leave in the pan. Add the peas to the sauce.

Set oven to 180°C.

Now we layer the mac. Add the deglazed liquor from the fish pan to the sauce. First we use macaroni, then add a small pepper from the jar and then some of the fish and 2–3 prawns, some crawfish tails and some cockles. Grate on some Cheddar and spoon over some sauce and layer again, seasoning as you go. Macaroni, pepper, fish, prawns, crawfish, cockles, Cheddar, sauce, season. When full, top up with sauce – the final layer will be Cheddar, of course. The sauce should be $\frac{2}{3}$ of the way up the casserole.

Now you're ready for the oven. Cook for 20 minutes until golden brown on top. If it colours too quickly lay a sheet of foil over and continue cooking.

Bring out the casserole carefully and allow to cool, adding slices and claw meat of lobster to the top.

Voila! You have one awesome mac and cheese.

SPANISH BAKED CHICKEN WITH CHORIZO AND SAFFRON

SERVES 4 OR 2 AS A LARGE MEAL

This recipe is vibrant and exciting and shines like the Mediterranean Sea with both colour and flavour. I have studied Spanish food and it is my belief that first and foremost we need the taste to be Spanish. I don't wish to be facetious here, but this is the ultimate mandate. So I have included ingredients from modern Spain that have been gathered as modern Spanish ingredients, but which were originally from the Americas and North Africa. We have the humble tomato, which is the fruit of Christopher Columbus's 1492 Spanish-commissioned voyage to find both 'pastures new' and to explore the West for ingredients. Columbus came back with a whole array of otherwise unknown ingredients to Spain until this point: yams, potatoes, cocoa, vanilla, and the humble tomato. The cinnamon was from an Asian jaunt for our conquistador and the passage of saffron was from Africa, where at its nearest point is only 18km from Spain. So inevitably the exchange of ingredients between the two countries is an old and trusted route. The orange is of course indigenous to Spain, but I have improved the orange flavour with the stock syrup, which both caramelises and deepens the orange flavours.

The key here is to brine your chicken breasts. Take a cup of water in a small/medium pan and simply boil and dissolve a tablespoon each of salt and sugar. Once dissolved, add cold water to just over halfway up the pan and refrigerate. Once cold just add the chicken breasts and leave covered in the fridge for 4–8 hours or overnight. This process is very good for whole chicken or rump steak or even salmon. The science behind it is called osmosis – the absorption of a liquid into a food – but in simple terms, the salt brings flavour and sugar brings caramelisation. It really is easy and will give a cheap chicken a £15 chicken flavour – the chicken keeps its moisture beautifully.

EQUIPMENT: Medium/large heavy-based pan
Small heavy-based pan – for orange stock

INGREDIENTS:
Brine:

- 2 chicken breasts in a plastic bag with buttermilk and tied – left in fridge for up to 4 hours
- 1 tbsp olive oil
- 1 medium onion – chopped
- 3–6 twigs of rosemary
- 110g chorizo – cut into chunks
- 1 carrot – chopped
- 1 red pepper – deseeded and chunky sliced
- 4mm slice of ginger – chopped
- 3 cloves of garlic – chopped
- Pinch of chilli flakes
- 1 tsp smoked paprika
- 400g tin of tomatoes, plus half the tin of water
- 400g tin of butterbeans – half drained
- 1 tsp capers
- Pinch of saffron threads
- 1 tbsp wine vinegar
- Splash of nam pla (optional) or salt
- 4 slices of reconstituted dried mushroom or fresh mushrooms
- Juice of 2 oranges and 2 level tsp of sugar – orange stock syrup
- 100g sharp mature Cheddar

METHOD:

Set oven to 180°C.

In the medium/large heavy-bottomed pan, pour in the olive oil on a medium heat. Add the onion and rosemary – stripped from the stem and discard the stalk. Let them just infuse for 4–5 minutes. Add the chorizo and allow the juices to flow orange-coloured before adding the carrot, pepper, ginger, garlic, chilli flakes, smoked paprika and let them cook down for 5 minutes. Add the tin of tomatoes with the tin of butterbeans – having poured half of the butterbean juice away first – capers, saffron, wine vinegar, nam pla, dried or fresh mushrooms, and stir them through. Bring them to a simmer, cover and let bubble for half an hour, allowing the flavours to mix.

Now make the orange stock syrup. In a small pan, mix the fresh orange juice and 2 tsp of sugar. Warm on a medium heat – just swirled, not touched – and reduce for 1–2 minutes. This intensifies the orange flavour and makes it taste Spanish.

Add this to the sauce now and mix through.

Note: no salt or pepper at this point, as the nam pla has a salting quality and the vinegar helps to season.

In a Pyrex-style glass casserole dish, or earthenware equivalent, pour in the sauce from the pan. Have a little look at seasoning now, but don't overdo it.

Take the chicken breasts from the brine, and wash and dry them on kitchen roll. Give them some olive oil and fresh ground pepper – lay them on top of the sauce – now ready for the oven. Lay on the bottom rack and cook for 45 minutes – keeping an eye on it.

Grate your Cheddar ready for the end.

At 40 minutes turn on grill.

At 45 minutes take out of the oven, lay the grated cheese on top and carefully grill until gratinéed and cooked to a golden crust of cheese.

Terminado!

You now have a very Spanish, smoky, tasty, saffron, orange-flavoured chicken dish.

Equally good with pork medallions – also brined in the same way.

Serve with either garlic mashed potatoes, traditional Spanish tortilla, pasta or rice.

STEAK AND KIDNEY COBBLER

SERVES 4 VERY WELL

I have always loved lambs' kidneys and I have been known to buy the kidneys with the suet still around them and just bake them for 10 minutes and then dig in with gusto. This is a great way to eat kidney by the way, with a dash of Dijon mustard to enhance the flavours. This all stems back to steak and kidney pie from the northern chip shop. The kidney has to earn its place in the chip shop pie, but in my steak and kidney they have a starring role with the shin beef – my favourite long-cooked beef cut. Everything is cut chunky. I have added chestnut mushrooms too, just halved and thrown in – nothing fancy here, cheesemeisters. What does the job here is the cobblers, or should I say dumplings, packed with deep-tasting Cheddar, cooked on top of the melting casserole for the last 45 minutes to expand and soak up the excess juices from the beer gravy. This is a steadying dish and quite rich, so be careful with the portions by topping the plate with some barely cooked broccoli or some other greens.

INGREDIENTS:
Casserole:
700g shin beef – cubed by the butcher
3 whole lambs' kidneys
3 medium onions
3–4 tbsp groundnut oil
1 tbsp beef dripping
Plain flour for dusting
8 chestnut mushrooms – halved
1 bottle/pint light beer
Fresh rosemary – chopped

Cobbler:
340g self-raising flour
140g cold butter
100g sharp Cheddar
5–8 sprigs of fresh rosemary – leaves chopped small
Juice of 1 lemon
Water to bind
Salt and pepper

EQUIPMENT:

2 heavy-based pans with lids

1 casserole dish or cast-iron casserole dish with lid

2 mixing bowls

Wooden spoon

Ladle

METHOD:

First chop your 3 onions, by halving lengthways and then slicing across the grain – not thick, not thin. In your pan have the groundnut oil ready and heated, throw in the onions and coat them in the oil. Put the pan lid on and cook on a medium heat on your hob, keeping an eye on the progress. It's good to let them catch a little and leave burnt bits on the bottom of the pan. After 45 minutes they should be well coloured. Decant the onions onto a plate and set aside. Save the pan for later – along with the burnt bits.

In your other pan have the beef dripping heated and slightly smoking. Add the chunky cut shin beef which you have dusted in plain flour. Add them in single layers so as not to overcrowd the pan. Colour them well and set aside.

In the first pan, pour some water from the tap to just about 2cm above the burnt bottom. Put straight on the heat and start scraping the bottom with the wooden spoon. When it comes to the boil the scraping will be easy. Throw in the onions and beef. Add half of the beer.

With the kidneys, you need to halve them lengthways and to carve out the white and quite hard centre – be careful here, it's tricky. Cut each half in half again making 3 quartered kidneys. Dust these kidney pieces in flour and add to the meat and onion. Throw in the halved mushrooms and sprigs of fresh rosemary. Bring it all to the boil and add water if you need to at this point. Add lots of pepper and very little salt.

The smells should all be there now.

Take your lidded casserole and transfer the casserole into the dish with a ladle. Cover with the lid and cook at 160°C for 2½ hours to allow the shin beef to soften and give up its flavour.

While the casserole is bubbling away you can prepare the cobblers.

In a mixing bowl, throw in the self-raising flour and grate in the cold butter and cheese. Mix them between your fingers to create a breadcrumb consistency. Add the chopped rosemary and mix again. Add the lemon juice and add just enough water – salt and pepper to your liking – to bring the mixture together into a dough, making the sides of the mixing bowl 'clean'. Cover and set aside.

After the 2½ hours in the oven, take out the casserole, uncover and add the rest of the beer and mix. Take a palm-sized piece of the cobbler and roll it your hands, creating a ball. This will make one of your cobblers. You will have enough dough to make 9 cobblers.

Arrange them around the outside of the casserole, leaving the last one to cover the middle area. They will expand, so don't overcrowd them. Cook them – uncovered – at 160°C again for 45 minutes to cook them through.

They should be well coloured and the casserole will smell amazing around the house.

This steak and kidney casserole is rich so be prepared to add a good green vegetable and be aware it is filling.

OX CHEEK OSSO BUCO AND CHEDDAR POLENTA

SERVES 4

When it comes to long-cooked and cheap cuts of beef, there are few cuts to challenge the ox cheek. The most used muscle on the ox and therefore needing a long cook to unlock a mouth-watering and beefy, soft and giving experience. This dish was originated in Lombardy in the 19th century; a rustic stew that delivers a no-nonsense but luxurious meal, combining the cheesy polenta with the citrus/garlicky gremolata, which makes this dish an all-time favourite of ours. The Italians hold the trump card on this type of dish because they care about nurturing flavour and long cooking. The key with this style of cooking is the balance of the richness with the soft acidity of the wine/cider/perry. It is well worth including in a special dinner and a worthy 'show-off' recipe. You can use ox tail instead of the cheek and cook it in exactly the same way. I cook this in a pressure cooker in 45 minutes, thus saving the 4 hours it would take to cook normally.

EQUIPMENT:

Pressure cooker or large, heavy-bottomed pan with lid

Medium, heavy-bottomed pan for polenta

Hand blender

INGREDIENTS:

1 tbsp groundnut oil – that can withstand high heat

2 ox cheeks – they really are a cheap cut

3 tbsp seasoned flour

2 tbsp olive oil

2 stalks of celery – roughly chopped

2 medium onions – roughly chopped

2 carrots – roughly chopped

2 450g tins of plum tomatoes

Half a pint of white wine or cider/perry – more if needed

4 sprigs of thyme

4 sprigs of rosemary

1 tbsp balsamic vinegar

Salt and pepper

Polenta:

3 parts water to 1 part polenta – for 4 – 170g Polenta

30g butter

80g sharp Cheddar – grated

Salt and pepper

Gremolata:

1 small/medium bunch of parsley – washed, dried and finely diced, thick stems discarded

Small pinch salt

Zest of 1 lemon – finely grated

1 clove garlic – finely chopped

METHOD:

Ready your pan for cooking the cheeks. I use groundnut oil here as it reaches a higher smoking point, so cooks at a higher temperature for searing. Heat the oil on medium, while you coat the cheeks with the seasoned flour. Turn up the heat to hot and when you are ready carefully lay the cheeks on the oil. Sear the cheeks well on both sides, colouring well and leaving behind a nice crispy bottom of the pan. Take out the ox cheek. Pour out the groundnut oil and replace with the olive oil on a medium heat. Add the mirepoix – onion, celery and carrot. Cook quickly and scrape the crispy bottom of the pan with your wooden spoon. After 5 minutes add the plum tomatoes and combine into the vegetables. Pour in the wine/cider/perry to just cover the mix. Drop in the cheeks and work them down the mix, so they are covered. Add the herbs at this point.

You are now ready to long cook the dish. If using a pressure cooker, bring up to pressure and cook for 45 minutes. If using your large pan, bring to the boil and then just simmer very lightly, with lid on for 4 hours, stirring occasionally.

In the meantime you can make your gremolata. Grate the lemon zest and the garlic, finely chop the parsley and combine all three. Set aside.

Once cooked, take out the ox cheeks and set aside carefully and discard the sprigs of herbs. It is now time to whizz the sauce with a hand blender until fairly smooth. The job here is to reduce the sauce by half, very slowly. Add the balsamic vinegar. It will take about an hour to reduce. Seasoning the sauce now takes priority. Good salt and freshly ground pepper will be important in bringing a nice balance of flavour.

Add the cheeks back to the sauce to come back to heat.

Making the Gremolata

In a mortar and pestle grind the parsley with the salt. Grind until fragrant and mushed a little. Add the garlic and grind again.

Finally add the lemon zest and grind until all are well combined. Spoon through to help combine.

Serve immediately for best results – it will keep for 3 days in the fridge.

Making the Polenta:

In your pan, throw in the polenta and water. Take your wooden spoon and start stirring as it heats through. After a while it will start to bubble. Turn down the heat to manage the bubbling and continue stirring. Add the grated Cheddar and stir into the mix. Taste and start seasoning with good salt and freshly ground pepper. When you are happy with the cheesy flavours and you are approaching 20 minutes of cooking, add the butter and allow to melt into the polenta. You are now ready to serve a tablespoon or so on each plate, accompanied by a half cheek and a liberal ladle of sauce. Top all this with 2–3 pinches of gremolata.

Enjoy!

AIGRETTES AND GOUGÈRES (V)

Here we have a curious rendering of Cheddar and choux pastry, combined to bring a crispy outer shell and a soft cheesy centre that can hardly be felt in the mouth. These French curiosities are a great addition to lots of meals or occasions, giving a sense of exclusivity to proceedings. In typically French style they are named aigrettes because of their shape, thinning at the end like an egret's neck. They can be either deep-fried to make the aigrette that sits in the supporting actor role next to the star, perhaps long-cooked beef or a hot dish of faggots, or they can be piped onto a greased baking tray and baked to become the French aperitif accompaniment gougères. They are perfectly formed to sit beautifully with red wine or champagne. The same recipe makes both of these superb culinary curiosities, little orbs of joy on the plate that are exquisitely easy to make.

EQUIPMENT:

Pan to deep fry
Pan to make the choux
Wooden spoon
Mixing bowl
Slotted spoon
Kitchen roll
Baking tray
Piping bag
Butter for greasing

INGREDIENTS:
Dry ingredients
90g plain flour
1 level tsp mustard powder
Pinch smoked paprika
A flash of salt
Pepper
75g butter
225ml water
3 medium eggs
60g sharp Cheddar – grated
Up to 1 tbsp oil for frying
Parmesan cheese – optional

METHOD:

Making a choux pastry is quite easy; it is just the combining of wet ingredients with dry ingredients and working the mixture with a wooden spoon so that it comes away from the edges of the pan.

So, weigh out the dry ingredients first in a bowl and set aside.

Combine the water and butter in the pan, then melt in the warming pan on a medium heat.

Throw in the dry ingredients and start working with the wooden spoon until well combined and it comes away from the edge of the pan. Take off the heat now and prepare your 3 eggs. Crack 1 egg at a time into the mix, working in until amalgamated. Now crack the second egg in there and repeat beating. When all three eggs are in there, add the grated Cheddar and watch it melt as you thoroughly mix it in. Give a good mix so you are happy with the smooth consistency. Season with salt and pepper and carefully fill your piping bag with the warm mixture, plugging the

end if need be to avoid any silly spillages.

Elastic-band the open end of the piping bag to secure and carefully lay in the fridge for up to an hour to cool and congeal; or put in the freezer for 20 minutes.

Aigrettes:

Heat the oil until a piece of bread fizzes when dropped in, then stabilise the heat to keep it around that temperature. Set a plate with kitchen roll to one side. With the piping bag in hand, hover it over the oil and squeeze out a 5cm piece of mixture and stop squeezing to then let it taper away from the piping back and lay comfortably in the sizzling oil. Repeat until you have about 6 in the pan. They are done when golden. Fish them out with a slotted spoon and drain on the kitchen roll. Repeat with another six, and so on. Present your food on the plate and lay your hot aigrette in pride of place next to the star of the plate, such as meat or fish.

Gougères:

Set the oven to 160°C.

Lightly grease the baking tray and have the cooled mixture in the piping bag ready. The gougères will grow slightly whilst cooking so be sure to have that in mind when spacing them out. With a circular motion, and a circumference of 5cm, lightly squeeze the piping bag to create a neat spiral. Breathe!

Repeat until you have filled the baking tray. Here you can finely grate over some Parmesan cheese as a topping to your gougères – totally optional – and cook in the oven for 15–20 minutes. They are cooked when beautifully puffed up and golden. Decant to a plate and serve to your guests, who will have been smelling the unctuousness for some time now!

Enjoy.

CHEDDAR AND MUSTARD YORKSHIRE PUDDING WITH SINGLE RIB OF BEEF

SERVES 4 VERY WELL

There are so many recipes for this ubiquitous pudding from Yorkshire, covering all measurements for the three ingredients and lots of different ideas on the fat to be used. The rules are simple and, for me, they should be. This pudding's alchemy goes back to the 1700s, where there were no scales in most houses and therefore the recipe would have been deliciously simple. I have created a recipe here that needs just a measuring jug, where we measure the 6 eggs in the jug and add to the mixing bowl, measure the milk to the same quantity and add to the bowl, and then add the same amount of flour and add to the bowl. This is the simple vehicle that carries this recipe. The difference here is that I am adding powdered mustard and Cheddar cheese, thus bringing a beautiful savoury edge to the famous table pleaser. In doffing my cap to this recipe I have decided to roast a single rib of beef over the pudding, which takes the same 20–25 minutes to cook as the pudding, dripping all its juices and further enriching the pudding.

I have credentials here too, as I was once thrown into the lion's den in a 'Yorkshire Pudding off', in competition against two Yorkshire chefs. Each of these chefs had multiple trophies for their puddings. Yes, they have annual competitions! The eight octogenarian Yorkshire women judges were a formidable panel, we were in the middle of Yorkshire and, needless to say, I had no chance; not even a sniff of a chance. A Lancashire lad taking on this deeply partisan county's Yorkshire pudding champs and the equally partisan jury. I deserved a good keelhauling; the barefaced cheek of it!

I used this very recipe and cooked it in a roasting tin swimming in smoking hot dripping from my local butcher. I whisked up my equal ingredients, added a tsp of salt and 3 tsp of powdered mustard and whisked in some bubbles. Straight from the hot oven and smoking like a peace pipe, the dripping was ready. I quickly poured my bubbly mix onto the fat and watched it fiercely bubble and splutter. I threw in 6 pieces of Cheddar and quickly it went back into the oven. The beef was already sealed and was awaiting the pudding on the top shelf of the oven, to then drip its goodly juices all over the pudding below during the following 25 minutes in the hot oven. In slid the tin and only then did I feel the pressure of cagey conversation and much rubbing of trophies, all designed to keep this Lancashire lad under the cosh. The puddings were in and the battle commenced. I genuinely felt the pressure but never showed it, and decided to stand in the car park with a beer.

After 25 minutes I returned to the engine room where my fellow competitors had already taken out their single Yorkshires and were guarding them with a twinkle of glee in their eyes. I approached my Rational oven to be met with … I can only describe it as a castle fortification of some immensity. My Yorkshire was massive! And the bed of the pudding had the crust of beefy savouriness. The oven welcomed me with a whoosh of steam and the aroma of a Caribbean barbecue. It was as perfect a Yorkshire as I could wish for.

Now for the biased jury's once-over. The three of us lined up, with me at the back (of course). My fellow Yorkshires were verily received with knowing nods and much talk in furrowed brows on how well they had been constructed, lots of crispy talk and much partisan congratulation was undertaken. I was next and chose to reveal my castle at the last moment, to a woo from the girls; all good there, then. The deliberation was slow and methodical to begin with, but then the jury was showing all the signs of a possible mutiny afoot. 'How can this be?' Looks abounded and much crunching and prodding unfolded throughout the coming minutes. The results were to be delivered in reverse.

The Sage Yorkshire Pudding was first out and was duly congratulated, leaving myself and Ben Cox of The Star in Sancton and his proudly stood, very high, examples of Yorkshireness. Ben is a champ with many medals from previous engagements. And in second place, was … (drum roll, please) Ben Cox!

Oh my god! I had won with my full-scale model of Skipton Castle! To be fair there was much congratulation from the panel of smiling Yorkshire ladies and firm handshakes from the ex champs as they too showed appreciation for my efforts.

That was a good day!

Needless to say now, this recipe is exactly the same as the Yorkshire on that day. So, just keep to the basics and you too will win your own competition.

EQUIPMENT:
Robust, non-stick roasting tin
Mixing bowl
Measuring jug
Electric whisk
Solid frying pan or skillet for the beef
Oven gloves!

INGREDIENTS:
6 really good eggs
The same amount of milk
The same amount of plain flour
1 tsp salt
3 tsp powdered mustard
6 'chunks' of sharp Cheddar
Dash of water
1 single rib of beef – it must be single
3 tbsp flour
1 level tsp rub of smoked paprika
1 tbsp dripping for sealing the meat
3 good tbsp of dripping for the roasting tin

METHOD:

Preheat the oven to 220°C and set the oven racks, with the highest level to take the beef and the lower one at level 2.

In your measuring jug crack the 6 eggs. Wherever they show on the ml scale, you will need to remember. Pour the eggs into the mixing bowl. Take the milk and measure exactly the same amount and pour into the mixing bowl. Pour the flour into the measuring jug to the same amount and add that to the mixing bowl. Add the salt and mustard powder and take the whisk to it, whizzing into a bubbly surface, and then set aside.

Heat up the skillet to very hot. This will take a couple of minutes, giving you time to flour-rub the beef. Coat the surface of the beef all over with the flour and rub in. Rub in the smoked paprika and you're ready to seal. Once the skillet is hot add the dripping and melt until smoking. Only then, carefully throw on the beef and seal on both sides – you can liberally salt it here too – until nicely coloured and a little crunchy. Carefully open the oven and lay the beef on the preset top-level rack of the oven – this will eventually be over the pudding.

Add a very quick turn of water to the batter and give it a final swirl.

This helps the pudding crispen.

Slide the roasting tray, laden with the dripping into the oven for 5 minutes. This heats the dripping to smoking point – and this is what you are after – a plume of smoke will waft from the oven as you open it carefully, wearing your oven gloves. Lay it on a heat-resistant surface – it will burn some surfaces, so be prepared with a trivet. Immediately pour in the batter mix and watch it splutter; this is perfect. Throw the chunks of cheese into the batter at equal distance from each other. Open the oven and carefully slide the roasting tray on the preset lower level. Close the oven and cook for 25 minutes – if the Yorkshire colours too quickly, turn the oven down a little, but keep the oven door closed until the full time is up.

Watching the Yorkshire rise is quite something.

After 25 minutes, carefully take out the massive Yorkshire and place on the trivet. Take out the beef and let it lay to rest a little. When you are all set to go, slice the beef thickly and garnish with good salt. Serve with potatoes, your chosen vegetables and great gravy.

This is a family hit. Just lay the Yorkshire on the table and the family will do the rest. Believe me!

CLASSIC MEAT LOAF

SERVES 4-6

Meat loaf is naturally a British meal in one, but I guess we all know it is from the States; more accurately it was Pennsylvania and dates back to 1870. So at some point this fab collection of fairly cheap and savoury ingredients found its way over the Atlantic. As I say, it became an affordable British way to feed the family and, at a guess, I would say that it could have come across with the GIs in the war perhaps. The addition of stale breadcrumbs adds to the affordability and also cuts back on the richness of meat and fat, making this meat loaf all about balance. Try making gravy from a small handful of the mince, thus matching the flavour of the loaf, and then pour seductively over a slice of loaf and silky mashed potatoes, making this a delightful winter warmer in any household. The addition of fine Cheddar here brings a taste of umami and therefore tickles those taste buds with savoury fusion.

EQUIPMENT:

Mixing bowl

Hand blitzer or liquidiser –
    for breadcrumbs

2lb loaf tin

Greaseproof paper

Medium heavy-bottomed pan and lid

Garlic press

INGREDIENTS:

15g butter

300g pork mince

300g beef mince

2/3 medium onions – chopped

1 carrot – chopped

1 celery stalk – chopped

2 cloves garlic – minced

40g stale breadcrumbs

200g fine Cheddar – 90g for
    mince, 110g for topping

1 tbsp Worcester sauce

1 tbsp mushroom ketchup –
    optional

2 tsp mustard powder

Lots of ground pepper

1 egg

METHOD:

Melt the butter in your pan. Add the chopped veg and cook down for 5 minutes. Put the lid on and cook for a further 5 minutes, so they soften nicely – don't colour the veg too much though. Take off the heat and allow to cool to touch temperature.

In your mixing bowl throw in the veg and the pork/beef mince. Add the breadcrumbs and start the flavouring with the mustard powder, Worcester sauce and mushroom ketchup. Cut the 90g of Cheddar into 2cm chunks and throw them in too. Grind over a lot of pepper and crack in the egg. Mix thoroughly by hand.

Line your loaf tin with the greaseproof – by using butter on the inside of the tin, allowing the greaseproof to stick. Pack in the meat loaf mix to the top and cook in the preheated oven for 45 minutes. Then lay the sliced 110g of Cheddar on top (see pic above) and cook for a further 15 minutes.

1 hour in total.

Allow to cool on a wire rack before unwrapping the greaseproof and confidently slicing the loaf.

DESSERTS

STP – STICKY TOFFEE PUDDING WITH DATE AND CHEDDAR ICE CREAM

SERVES 4

The famous sticky toffee pudding – smooth toffee sauce poured over a perfect toffee sponge accompanied by ice cream, fulfilling the hot-cold style of dessert par excellence. But is the STP always sticky? I'm not so sure. I have some credentials here, as I was in competition with the two most qualified STP chefs in the UK, in a challenge to find the best example of this batter pudding. My competitors were famous for their STPs: Sharrow Bay Hotel in Ullswater and the Cartmel STP Company; both in Cumbria. I really had little or no chance in this company, but the one thing I had on my side was a free hand to choose whatever ingredients that suited me – whereas my fellow competitors were (pardon the pun) 'stuck' to their recipes. My lightbulb moment was to add cinder toffee to my batter just prior to baking – my idea being that it would either have a toffee crunch or it would melt and add to the toffee experience. My chances had improved about a thousandfold with this addition; it was quickly falling into the bracket of a 'brainstorm moment'. The pudding had the 'sticky' nailed, actually sticking to the palate for a second, and slowing everything down as you conjure with the world of STICKY. It was a triumphant decision and this recipe is here for you, accompanied by the marvellous and equally triumphant Cheddar ice cream (see recipe on page 171), making this dessert a marvel. I won out on the day and had the culinary buzz of my life on the lapping edges of Ullswater – a great day indeed.

EQUIPMENT:
Medium heavy-bottomed pan
Deep bowl for mixing
2lb loaf tin
Hand blitzer or liquidiser
Small bowl for the dates

INGREDIENTS:
Sauce:
115g butter
75g golden castor sugar
40g dark brown sugar
130ml double cream
Dates:
200g dates – finely chopped
1 level tsp baking powder
300ml boiling water

Pudding Batter:
60g butter – room temperature
  and soft
80g golden castor sugar
80g dark brown sugar
2 medium eggs
Vanilla essence
175g plain flour – sifted
70g cinder toffee

METHOD:
First make the sauce, by putting all the sauce ingredients in a pan and mixing with a wooden spoon while it comes to the boil. Turn down heat now and simmer for 10 minutes to reduce to the right consistency. Grease the bread tin liberally with butter and pour half of the sauce into the bread tin. Freeze this until needed.

Throw the dates into a bowl with the baking powder. Now add the 300ml of boiling water, mix and leave for 20 minutes.

In the meantime, you can make the batter. With your deeper bowl, add the softened butter and the two sugars. Start to work with the wooden spoon – this takes elbow grease, as you need to work it into a light and creamy mix. Add the eggs and a dash of vanilla and mix to a smooth consistency before adding the sifted flour and the dates with their water. Mix this together before blitzing in a liquidiser for 30 seconds, or hand-blending with the appropriate hand mixer for 2 minutes, until smooth.

In a bowl and with the end of a rolling pin, smash up the cinder toffee into 1cm chunks.

Preheat the oven to 180°C.

Take the bread tin out of the freezer. Pour the cinder toffee into the sauce at the last minute, before pouring the batter into the bread tin on top of the frozen sauce.

Bake in the oven for 30 minutes until fully cooked. Let it cool a little.

After 15 minutes of cooking, take your ice cream from the freezer to acclimatise and be ready to place on the plate. Reheat the remaining sauce.

Have your plates ready and carefully slice a portion per plate. I use an electric knife. Pour over a spoonful of hot sauce onto each portion before adding a good scoop of the (already made) Cheddar ice cream (page 171).

Proudly serve.

And look forward to slowing down into STICKY world!

Enjoy.

CHEDDAR ET POMME TARTE FINE (V)

The partnership of apple and cheese is quite amazing. I have studied this subject a lot and the sweet of the apple sits really well with the salty savoury cheese – if it is well balanced. This recipe is typically French and I have a penchant for this dessert when Frenchside. It was the addition of Cheddar that blew this recipe skyward – it is that good! The Cheddar cheese ice cream then sends this recipe stratospheric – so if you have an ice cream maker, try it. A hot tarte fine with freezing cold Cheddar ice cream melting all over it is amazing. It is the saltiness of the cheese that makes it taste like salted caramel – but better! This recipe will easily roll over to the next day or keep in fridge for 3 days.

EQUIPMENT:

Baking tray to take an 18–20cm circle of pastry

Grater

Fine Sieve

Rolling pin

Blow torch (optional)

INGREDIENTS:

Block of shop-bought puff pastry

Plain flour

Egg wash

2–3 British apples

50g vintage Cheddar

Lemon juice

Icing sugar

10g melted butter

METHOD:

Set oven to 180°C. Take the puff pastry and lightly flour the work surface. Roll to the thickness of a pound coin. With a pan lid or something circular, make an 18–20cm circle in the puff pastry and cut out the circle. Keep the remaining pastry in the fridge. Lift the circle of pastry by rolling onto a rolling pin. Flour your baking tray lightly. Then lay the pastry in the middle of the tray. With a sharp knife get ready to score the pastry disc with a line 1cm in from the edge (by spinning the tray) all the way around the circle. Just score it, nothing more. Then lightly fork the inner circle – not the outside 1 cm. Wash with the egg wash and put into the preheated oven for 13–15 minutes to just golden up. You will be cooking the pastry again so take care not to overdo it. Once on the work surface, take a teaspoon and, holding it horizontally with the back of the spoon to the pastry, glide it around the inside edge of the pastry. Push the inside edge down as you slide the spoon around the inner circle, to push the inside down and leave the 1cm border edge still proud – like a wall around the tart. Then press the entire inner circle down the same.

Take the cheese and grate it lightly over the inner circle – if any flops over the edge, bring it back into the inner circle. Take the apples and halve them from top to bottom. Put them in a bowl and drizzle the lemon juice over. Core the halves – top to bottom again – by going in with a sharp knife and cutting out the core with an angled cut, down one side of the core, then the other, so they join in the middle and the core comes free in a Toblerone shape. Discard the core. Now with your nice sharp knife – not too big a knife – thinly slice the apples, top to bottom again.

It is here where you can spoon over some apple sauce onto the puff pastry disc – this is optional.

Lightly press down the Cheddar to create a level ground for the apples.

Lay the apples on top of the cheese – in a fan (see pic) nice and neat. Brush over lightly with melted butter. Sieve lightly with icing sugar.

Cook in the oven for 15–18 minutes until cooked and bubbling.

You can sieve over some more icing sugar now and blowtorch, if you have one (optional). All done.

This recipe is easy. You just need to be pragmatic with the scoring, forking of the pastry and fanning the apples.

Keep the rest of the puff pastry to make another one – shop-bought puff pastry can be used again.

APPLE SOUFFLÉ (V)

MAKES 6 SOUFFLÉS

Souffles, the arch-enemy of most home cooks, the antithesis to an enjoyable cooking session for friends and family; where all the rules of culinary knowledge collide into a wall of white noise; where the brain turns any wording into a stream of firecrackers bouncing down a Chinatown street amidst some mysterious dream of ceremonial dragons and total chaos.

Well, listen up, my cheesemeister friends, and set the brain to receive with clarity. With this knowledge you could find yourself making soufflés on a much more regular basis. The whole process is set up as stages. You have one pan to make the base flavour. You split 3 eggs to whites and yolks. You have your electric hand whisk to hand. You have your soufflé ramekins to hand too, lightly greased and coated with castor sugar.

Easy.

These particular soufflés use the apple as the ramekin, so it's even easier. I use a dash of Somerset apple brandy from 'Burrow Hill' near Langport in Somerset, but the addition of Calvados is just as acceptable – and gorgeous, so there are less excuses now to flick past this page as 'totally not!'

EQUIPMENT:

Dessert spoon

1 small, heavy-based pan

Potato masher

Electric hand whisk

Baking sheet

Sieve

INGREDIENTS:

6 Braeburn apples

2 tbsp golden castor sugar, plus 1 tbsp for the egg whites

3 eggs – split into whites and yolks

Dash of Calvados

Juice of 1 lemon

METHOD:

One apple per person here, guys. Take each apple and sit it on your work surface. You are looking for the apple to sit flat, and therefore you might need to just shave off part of the bottom to bring a flat sitting apple.

Cut the apple ⅓ up from the bottom, leaving ⅔ as surplus.

Take your dessert spoon and, leaving a 4mm edge of apple intact around the circumference of the base, press in the spoon, lightly at first, and then with more effort. Scoop out the inner of the apple, leaving the 'skin' of the apple 4mm thick all around the apple-base 'ramekin' – this will be your serving cup. Squeeze over the lemon juice to stop discolouring and a dash of Calvados to flavour. Set aside.

Peel and core 2 of the surplus apples, then chunky chop them and throw into your small pan. Add 3 tbsp water from the tap and 2 level tbsp of castor sugar. Give it a swirl and allow the apples to break down. If it dries up add 1 or 2 tablespoons of water to bring it back. Once broken down, mash it with your potato masher. Set aside to cool.

Set the oven to 180°C.

Break the eggs and separate – the key here is no yolk in the whites bowl. Save 2 yolks for the apples, but only add them when the apples have cooled a little.

Take the hand whisk and whizz the whites up to soft peaks – about 1 minute. Then add the extra 1 tbsp of sugar and whizz to finish the whites to solid and glossy peaks.

Now you should have a pan of mashed apples, a bowl of whipped egg whites, and 6 apple cups.

Take a tablespoon and spoon a quarter of the egg white into the apple and egg yolks, then mix thoroughly.

Then add all the egg white to the pan, but now you are looking to 'fold' the mixture with the tablespoon. A figure-of-eight motion is good here, lifting the apples off the bottom and carefully folding through the egg white. This should take just 45 seconds – don't kill all the air in the egg white.

You're now ready to spoon the soufflé into the apple cups. Take a cup and add a spoonful of soufflé mixture. Turn the spoon upside down and use the bend of the spoon to smooth the egg into the apple. Repeat as you turn the apple and spoon. It will only take about 2–3 spoons and you'll be there. Set the apple onto a baking tray and repeat the process with all the other apples.

Place the loaded baking sheet in the middle of the pre-heated oven and cook for 15–18 minutes. Watch them rise and pat yourself on the back.

The time in the oven will guarantee they are cooked and they shouldn't fall until the diner pushes in their spoon.

Well done, you!

FIERY GINGER CAKE AND RASPBERRY RIPPLE ICE CREAM

SERVES 6

So, here we have the culmination of the unlikeliest of ingredients: ginger and Cheddar cheese. It is a match brought together for a couple of interesting reasons. Firstly there is a kinship with Cheddar and ice cream, a savoury saltiness, matching the slight sweetness of the ice cream custard; a balance. This is the same as salted caramel ice cream, but way better! You have the saltiness, but then the added taste of that Cheddar from the 'top of the lasagne' flavour – the one we all crave and fight over, the crusty pay-off from your great work in the kitchen. Then, to trump that, there is the extra umami we are bringing to this delicious ice cream party, that fifth dimension of flavour coming from the ginger and the cheese. Light the blue touch paper and ready yourself for the Cheddar and fiery ginger experience, you have a palate supernova right there. You know that feeling you had when you first saw the Michelangelo ceiling fresco in the Sistine Chapel? That's the reaction to this mind-bending dessert. All you need is an ice cream maker – or you could stir and freeze over 3 hours.

Oh, and you will need the curiosity of a prowling jaguar …

EQUIPMENT:
small/medium heavy-bottomed pan

A large bowl

Balloon whisk

Prepared 2lb loaf tin (either lined with greaseproof paper or a loaf case added)

INGREDIENTS:
Fiery ginger cake:

225g wholemeal flour

10g ground ginger

10g mixed spice

1 (flat) tsp bicarbonate of soda

1 (flat) tsp baking powder

50g soft brown sugar

100g unsalted butter

175g black treacle

50g golden syrup

5g cumin seeds

150ml milk

3 eggs (medium) beaten

40g stem ginger – thinly sliced

Makes a 2lb loaf cake. Cake is much better if it can be cooled wrapped in greaseproof paper and then tinfoil and left for a couple of days. The flavours and stickiness of this cake will develop. It is also great served warm with ice cream!

You will need a small pan, a large bowl, balloon whisk, prepared 2lb loaf tin (either lined with greaseproof paper or a loaf case added).

METHOD:

Pre-heat oven to 160°C.

Melt butter, treacle and syrup on a low heat. Remove from the heat, gradually beat in the milk, then allow the mixture to further cool whilst weighing and preparing the remainder of the ingredients.

Put all of the dry ingredients into a large mixing bowl Add the beaten eggs to the cooled liquid with the stem ginger.

Pour the liquid into the dry ingredients and use the balloon whisk to mix and whisk together.

Once mixed well, pour into the prepared loaf tin.

Cook in the centre of the oven for 40–45 minutes, or until a knife inserted into the middle of the cake comes out clean. I usually test this at 40 minutes as you don't want to overcook this beauty!

Once cooked, remove from the oven and place on a cooling rack for 15 minutes to cool slightly before removing the cake from the loaf tin.

Place the cake still in its loaf case or baking paper on the cooling rack and enjoy the aroma – but leave it alone!

Once fully cooled, wrap and store for 24–48 hours – if you can last that long!

All you need now is the ice cream …

CHEDDAR ICE CREAM
PLUS 3 FLAVOURINGS

WE ALL SCREAM FOR ICE CREAM

Ice cream, the domain of Italians, where generations have proudly produced artisan and creamy, well-balanced and seriously (in Italy they are fiercely serious about their food) great ice cream. Secret recipes abound in the gelato parlours of Sicily – ingredients and techniques are passed down the family like precious classic Lamborghinis! Now loved just as much in the UK, some of us even search out the artisan, handmade, farmhouse ice cream – that hits those Italian buttons. Whatever your tipple the ice cream market in the UK is worth £1.1bn per year, and we are even loving the stuff in winter too! So, I thought we'd have a go at Cheddar ice cream in the hope that my curiosity would pay off. The cheese is creamy and savoury, so there are qualities there to help a good recipe along. I just need to take a chance and listen to my instincts here and hopefully bring some class to the table, taking Cheddar ice cream to the next level – the level that surprises the sceptic, stopping us short in our culinary tracks; in the hope of hijacking the salted caramel camp and taking it to the savoury boot camp; to punch a hole in its wafer and blow a raspberry (ripple) at tradition. This is where I want to take it. I have given myself an ice cream headache with this recipe, trying to make it work for the home kitchen. So, with our ice cream maker bowls in the freezer, cold and ready to rumble, let's churn.

The key here is to master the art of dry frying our grated Cheddar; yes, melting it and releasing the oils whilst watching it bronze in a dry, non-stick frying pan. We then have to master the careful 'enticing' of the cooling Cheddar 'disc' from the pan with our trusty spatula, letting it cool further and crispen up. If we can master this then the rest is fairly straightforward. So, join me with this recipe and hopefully you'll be knocking up the next 'must-have' in ice cream flavours yourself.

EQUIPMENT:

Ice cream maker – with bowl well frozen

Heavy-bottomed pan for the custard

Non-stick 24cm frying pan

Trusty spatula – plastic to protect the non-stick pan

Grater

Kitchen roll

Mixing bowl

Sieve

INGREDIENTS:

ICE CREAM

200ml whole milk

150ml double cream

Vanilla pod

3 egg yolks

80g golden castor sugar

Yellow food colouring – optional

50g sharp Cheddar – grated

METHOD:

In a heavy-bottomed saucepan, throw in the milk and cream and food colouring (optional). Start warming through on low/medium heat. Split the vanilla pod down the middle and throw into the milk/cream. Warm up to the point of boiling and take straight off the heat. Leave to cool for 20 minutes.

While this is cooling, crack the eggs into a clean bowl. Add the sugar and whisk for 2 minutes by hand to a silky, ribbony consistency. Set aside.

Remove the vanilla from the milk. Pour the cooled milk/cream mix into the ribbony yolks slowly, whilst continually whisking to combine. Then pour all back into the pan and cook again – but on low! – for 10 minutes, continually stirring with a spoon until it thickens – to cover the back of the spoon nicely.

Let this cool completely, before pouring into the ice cream maker and stir as per the operation instructions of your device. When the ice cream is coming together, after 5 minutes, break up the Cheddar disc (recipe below) into pieces and throw into the ice cream mix. Let the ice cream come together and congeal now.

Voila, you now have the opportunity to taste a little piece of heaven!

FLAVOURING THE ICE CREAM:

RASPBERRY RIPPLE
180g fresh raspberries
30g castor sugar
Juice of 1 fresh orange

In a medium heavy-based pan, throw in the raspberries, sugar and orange juice. Bring to the boil and simmer until thickened a little. Sieve through a fine sieve into a ramekin and reserve until set, ready for swirling through the fresh ice cream with a spoon – one or two swirls only. Decant into an airtight container and freeze until needed.

GINGER:

When the ice cream is coming together after 5 minutes in the ice cream maker, throw in 3 balls of stem ginger (diced) and a good pinch of fresh ground ginger and the broken crispy Cheddar disc. Continue with the ice cream process until fully made. Decant into an airtight container and freeze until needed.

CHOCOLATE:

In a double boiler, melt 100g milk chocolate. Once melted, add the milk/cream mixture from above and continue as described. After 5 minutes in the ice cream maker, add the broken Cheddar disc and continue until ice cream is ready. Decant into an airtight container and freeze until needed.

Il Gelato Club Segreto.

CRISPY COOKED CHEESE DISC:

On your 24cm dry (no oil) frying pan, heat on medium/high. Drop on the grated Cheddar and spread until well distributed around the pan. It will start to sizzle and give up its oil. Just watch here, no touching. You may be able to angle the pan to distribute the cheese evenly, but no touching. Turn down a little, so it's not so fierce now. After 4 minutes or so you will see and smell the cheese bronzing. This is what you want. Take from the heat and put the pan on something cold, like a marble work surface or sink drainer, for 1–2 minutes while it is cooling – don't go in too soon! With a spatula, just try to lift the edge of the cheese from the pan. It will still be hot, but cooling nicely. Lift this edge with your fingers and continue sliding the spatula under and across the bottom of the pan, thus releasing the cheese, until you are now holding a disc of honeycombed and fairly hot cheese. Lay this on some kitchen roll and top with more kitchen roll. Briefly lay the bottom of the pan on the 'kitchen-rolled' cheese to flatten. Once the oil is mopped on the kitchen roll, take away and discard. Leave the cheese to cool and crispen up on a cool surface.

CHEDDAR BAKEWELL (V)

SERVES 8

If ever there was a favourite vintage dessert that excites me just at the thought of eating it, it's the Bakewell. Evoking sunny afternoons by the Wye River in Derbyshire, alive with large trout, and Bakewell's vibrant high street alive with 'original' Bakewell shops. The only criticism I would have is that sometimes it can be a shade too sweet. Too much sugar. Especially when they decide to ice the top, double sweet is the call. My mind started working on this recipe ages ago and it seemed to me that there was room here for Cheddar to temper the sweetness with a back note of saltiness and the addition of a savoury depth. This recipe has been tried and tasted many times over and is a mainstay in my household – much to the delight of friends and family. I have been extolling the virtues of Cheddar as a flavour enhancer instead of a flavour dominator and the Cheddar Bakewell walks away with the title in this category. The Cheddar brings a crunch to the pastry party too, making it nice and short. Try it out and you'll have to agree that the balance works. Balance is everything to me. And Cheddar Bakewell has a ring to it. This dessert will be a smash!

EQUIPMENT:

25cm, loose-bottomed, fluted tart tin

2 mixing bowls

Rubber spatula

Wooden spoon

A method for blind baking – either rice and greaseproof or baking balls and greaseproof

1 cup of hot water

Zester tool

Sieve

Rolling pin

Hand whisk

INGREDIENTS:

PASTRY:

200g plain flour – sifted

60g unsalted butter at room temperature

60g sharp Cheddar – grated

30g icing sugar

Zest of 1 lemon

Milk to bind

Egg wash

FRANGIPANE:

150g softened butter

130g castor sugar

3 large eggs

150g ground almonds

Dash of almond essence

80g sharp Cheddar – grated

100g flaked almonds

1 jar damson jam (optional), any jam of your preference

METHOD:

First we need to make the pastry, so take your mixing bowl and combine the sifted flour with icing sugar and cubed butter. Work it with your fingers to make a breadcrumb consistency. Add the grated Cheddar and the lemon zest. Then add the lemon juice and bind together with a tbsp or two of milk. Bring together into a ball that 'cleans' the sides of the mixing bowl. Wrap in cling wrap and set aside in the fridge.

Set the oven to 180°C.

Take the loose-bottomed tart tin and butter it well. Have your flour and rolling pin to hand for rolling the cooled pastry. On a lightly floured surface roll out the pastry to the thickness of a pound coin. Flour lightly and 'load' your rolling pin with the pastry by rolling it onto the pin. Offer the pastry up to the tart tin and cover the tin with the pastry. Work the pastry into the buttered tin but take care not to stretch the pastry. Just be careful. Leave some pastry overlapping. Set the loaded tin onto a baking tray and line the pastry with the greaseproof paper. Pour in the rice or baking beans and bake in the middle of the oven for 15 minutes. Take the greaseproof and beans away. Egg-wash the base of the pastry and cook for a further 10 minutes, until 'lined' with egg wash.

While the pastry is cooking we need to prepare the frangipane. In the mixing bowl cream together the sugar and butter with your wooden spoon until fluffy and pale. This takes some elbow grease but is worth it in the end. Add the 3 eggs and mix thoroughly – with a hand whisk now. Add the ground almonds, almond essence and grated Cheddar, and then mix through to combine. Set aside.

Take out the pastry. Set up with a tablespoon, the hot water and jam ready to line the base of the Bakewell. Spoon on the jam, using as much or as little as you think you need, without making the layer over thick.

Turn the oven down to 160°C.

Fill the pastry with the frangipane mix. Use the back of a spoon dipped in hot water to distribute the frangipane evenly. Top the frangipane with the flaked almonds, covering any blemishes showing jam so the tart appears uniform and ready for the oven. Cook in the middle of the oven again for 30–35 minutes until golden. You will smell the almonds and the Cheddar through the kitchen. Lovely.

Allow to cool a little before standing a tin on your work surface. Lay the Bakewell on the tin and watch the side fall away, revealing the tart on the bottom of the tin, ready to slice and serve up. Serve hot or cold.

CHEDDAR ICE CREAM ARCTIC ROLL (V)

Back in the 1970s, as I was growing up and enjoying my food, I was served up an Arctic roll at my grandparents' house at the weekend. The casing of cake, resembling a Swiss roll but filled with cold and delicious vanilla ice cream, was like magic to me. The ship-in-the-bottle conundrum for a young 10-year-old: 'Just how do they do that Grandma?' 'It's a secret, Sean. It's food magic and is a new product in the supermarket.' All these years later, we are making one and unlocking the magic for the home cook. We're even pushing the Arctic roll into the future a little by utilising my Cheddar ice cream. There are a few components here that need some thought and time to gather together, but believe me it's worth all the effort for your 10-year-old grandson or indeed your own kids for a weekend treat or a birthday.

It turns out that the Arctic roll was brought to these shores by a Czechoslovakian by the name of Dr. Ernest Velden, who first set up shop in Eastbourne in 1968. The Arctic roll was a really popular dessert within my circle of friends, as it was nationwide. During the 1980s more than 40km (25 miles) of Arctic roll was 'rolling' off the production line, per day. Retro puds are enjoying a renaissance in restaurants, I'm told, so this one should fit in that category very well.

EQUIPMENT:

Ice cream maker – with frozen bowl

Swiss roll baking tray

Electric hand whisk

Greaseproof paper

Knob of butter

Cling wrap

Sieve

2 pans to take 2 glass bowls for double boiler

2lb loaf tin

Mixing bowl

Rubber spatula

INGREDIENTS:

Sponge:

2 medium eggs

60g castor sugar

70g plain flour

15g cocoa powder

Ice Cream:

As per recipe for Vanilla Cheddar Ice Cream (page 171)

60g milk chocolate

50g white chocolate

15 cherries

Smooth cherry jam

Icing sugar

METHOD

Sponge:

In a mixing bowl, crack the eggs and add the sugar. Mix with the hand whisk for up to 3 minutes until doubled in volume and light and airy. Sift in the plain flour and cocoa together and fold all together with a rubber spatula.

Set oven to 180°C.

Lightly butter the Swiss roll tin and lay over a measured piece of greaseproof paper, pushing it onto the butter to secure the bottom and corners. Lightly butter the greaseproof 'top' and pour in the sponge mix. Spread to fill the tin to all four corners.

Slide the sponge into the oven for 7 minutes.

In the meantime, measure off another piece of greaseproof to cover the tin and set aside on a bread board, ready for the cooked sponge. As soon as the sponge comes out of the oven, turn it out (turn upside down) onto the prepared greaseproof on the breadboard. Take away the tin quickly. With the greaseproof now either side of the hot sponge, roll up tightly into a roll – widthways, not lengthways – and set aside.

Ice Cream:

This is made according to the recipe for Vanilla Cheddar Ice Cream (see page 171). On a 50cm piece of cling wrap, spoon the ice cream onto one end of the cling wrap. Carefully start rolling the ice cream in the cling wrap, away from you, to essentially make a Christmas cracker of ice cream. Twist the ends closed and nestle in the freezer in a 2lb loaf tin, lined with scrunched up newspaper to cradle the ice cream cracker. Freeze.

Constructing the Arctic Roll:

Unwrap the sponge and take off the top greaseproof paper and discard. Use the cherry jam to cover the sponge lightly, pushing it around with the back of a spoon into all corners.

Take the frozen ice cream out of the freezer and unwrap the cling wrap quickly. Lay the ice cream on the shorter end of the sponge (it should be the same size) and tightly roll up the sponge/ice cream to make a Swiss roll. Carefully gauge the cut on

the sponge to bring the two ends snugly together, then lay the Swiss roll on the join to secure, for now.

Take cling wrap and carefully wrap up snugly before slipping back into the freezer for later.

On the Day:

Take the wrapped Arctic roll from the freezer, place it on the serving plate, and bring up to a temperature that allows a knife to cut through. This is critical and should be watched closely. In the meantime take 2 pans and ⅓ fill with water. Place a glass bowl onto each pan to create double boilers. Bring to the boil and then simmer each pan. Throw the white chocolate into one pan and the milk chocolate into the other. Allow to melt down completely. Take a fork and douse the Arctic roll with a trickle (left and right). To decorate this roll 'a la photo', dip your cherries in the white chocolate and place on greaseproof paper to set. Use the set cherries to adorn the roll and you have a finished, futuristic/retro Arctic roll to amaze the kids with.

RETRO CHOCOLATE BAKED ALASKA (V)

WITH A TWIST

The retro pud is back and I'm guessing we all remember the amazing baked Alaska – the near impossible kitchen fable of cooking ice cream in a fiercely hot oven. Surely this is a recipe for disaster! Indeed no, would be the reply from the far end of the kitchen as chef devours the whole dessert in a sugar frenzy of some magnitude. Chocolate sponge cake bearing the weight of my chocolate/Cheddar ice cream and a rendering of glossy, lightly sugared meringue, thrown into the 230°C oven for 4 minutes, is all it takes to bring back the retro pud of choice for me.

The name 'baked Alaska' was apparently first used at Antoine's, a restaurant in New Orleans, by its originator and chef de cuisine Antoine Alciatore in 1867, to honour the acquisition by the United States of Alaska from the Russian Empire on March 10th that year. Well, I didn't think it was that old!

We have been surprising guests and children with this wondrous dessert ever since. I have been very aware of the sugar content and have knocked back the amounts accordingly and I think it works well, and in conjunction with the choc/Cheddar ice cream and a fountain of raspberries, we are in for a dessert treat.

EQUIPMENT:

Base of a 21cm spring form circular baking tin

Swiss roll baking tray

Electric hand whisk

Rubber spatula

Electric knife – optional

3 mixing bowls

Sieve

INGREDIENTS:

Base:

3 eggs

80g castor sugar

100g self-raising flour

20g cocoa

Cream:

200ml double cream

Meringue:

4 egg whites

60g castor sugar

35g cinder toffee – smashed into small pieces

Punnet of raspberries

METHOD:

Set oven to 180°C.

In a mixing bowl, throw in the 3 eggs and the sugar and whip to double in volume – 3 minutes approximately. Sift over the self-raising flour and cocoa and take your rubber baking spatula to fold the ingredients together, so the colour is uniform but still light and airy. Butter your Swiss roll tray and 'stick' your greaseproof paper – cut to size – to the butter, to secure in place. Pour over the sponge mix and spread uniformly. Slide into the middle of the oven for 12 minutes. Take from the oven and cool. Once cooled, take the Swiss roll tin away and lay the sponge and greaseproof on your worktop. Offer up the base of your spring form tin and lightly draw a line around it with a sharp knife – making sure not to go straight through. This is a guide for you to cut a smaller circle just 2cm in from the scored edge. You should now have a circle of sponge 2cm smaller than the base. Lay on the base, cling wrap and set aside.

Cream:

In a bowl, whisk up the double cream to set peaks – be careful not to turn it into butter! Set aside.

Ice Cream:

Take your prepared chocolate/Cheddar ice cream (see recipe on pages 171/2) from the freezer for 10 minutes, to soften slightly from frozen.

Meringue:

In a non-metal bowl, whisk up the egg whites to soft peaks. Slowly add the sugar, as you are whisking, to bring to glossy stiff peaks. Set aside.

Turn oven up to 230°C.

Construction:

Have all your components together: base with sponge, raspberries, choc/Cheddar ice cream, whipped cream, meringue.

Have 2 dessert spoons set in a glass with hot water.

Firstly unwrap the base and sponge. Daub on a tbsp of whipped cream to cover the sponge circle. Throw on the raspberries in a single layer – leaving a circle uncovered with raspberries in the middle, to take the ice cream.

Now, cut your ice cream into 4cm blocks x 3. Stack them on top of each other. Cover the ice cream with whipped cream. Sprinkle over the cinder toffee. Then cover/stick the raspberries to the cream, to cover all the ice cream.

With your hot spoons, take a spoonful and offer it up to the dessert. Use the other spoon to push the meringue off this spoon and onto the dessert, thus sticking to the raspberries. Repeat the spoons method until the dessert is completely covered – this is fun – making sure there are no gaps and the appearance is like an igloo.

Slide the Alaska into the hot oven on an upturned baking sheet – so it is flat. Be careful here. Cook for 4 minutes until golden and attractive.

Carefully extract from the oven and ready yourself with an electric knife – optional – or carefully slice through with a suitable knife.

A SOMERSET, CHEDDAR-CRUSTED APPLE PIE (V)

SERVES AN ARMY

What is finer than apple pie, steaming from the oven as hot as a volcano and oozing appley gorgeousness around the house? Drizzled or drowned in homemade custard, whatever your tipple, nothing is finer in my mind. The traditionalist in me has had to include this Cheddar-crusted version, a version used for hundreds of years. The addition of Cheddar smartens up the flavour and helps knock back any unnecessary big sweetness, giving a delicate saltiness and an underlying savoury edge. I also add cider to the shortcrust pastry instead of milk, making this pie a true Somerset apple pie. You may not have encountered one before, so I thought we'd make one together. There's no need to be using fine, clothbound cheese here, but a good, sharp block of Cheddar will suffice perfectly. If, like me, you love to cook traditional recipes, you'll have some cathartic fun with this one.

EQUIPMENT:

Great plate pie dish
Heavy-based pan for the apples

Mixing bowl
Scales
Grater

Egg/pastry brush
Baking sheet
Tinfoil

INGREDIENTS:

4 Braeburn apples – unpeeled,
  cored and roughly chopped
2 lemons – for zest and juice
80g castor sugar
100g sultanas
100g Cheddar – big cubes
20g butter

Pastry:

220g plain flour – sifted
60g butter – cold and cubed
60g Cheddar – grated
Zest of half a lemon
Cider to bind
1 egg – beaten, for egg wash

METHOD:

Let's make the pastry first. In the mixing bowl, sift the flour and add the 60g of cubed butter and grated Cheddar. Mix through your fingers until it resembles breadcrumbs. Add the lemon zest and then bind the mixture together with a few tbsps of cider – the amounts vary so just add small amounts until you leave a clean bowl behind – wrap with cling wrap and put in the fridge for 10 minutes only.

While the pastry cools we will make the filling. Take your pan and add the 20g of butter, melt it down and add your roughly chopped apples. Add the lemon juice to stop any discolouring and bring up to a good heat. Cook these apples now for 4–5 minutes only – you just want to give them a start as Braeburns only need this. Tip them into the mixing bowl and add the sugar and sultanas – use a few more sultanas if you like them. Add the chunky cubes of Cheddar and the zest of a lemon. Give it all a good mix with your hands and set aside.

Now for the rolling of pastry and lining the pie dish.

Once out of the fridge, unwrap the pastry and lightly flour your work surface. Take the pastry and cut it in half, keeping one half for the bottom and one for the top of the pie. Bottom first. Butter the pie dish liberally and set aside nearby. Roll out the pastry to about the thickness of a pound coin and bigger than the pie dish – check by putting the pie dish over the pastry. Load the rolling pin with the pastry and offer it up to the greased pie dish. Unload the rolling pin neatly over the dish and snugly fit the pastry in there, leaving an overlap of spare pastry.

With your hands now, fill the pie with the apple/sultana/cheese filling until you have a good mound above the edge of the dish. Take the tines of a fork and press them in around the edge of the pie pastry. Egg-wash the tining. Set aside nearby.

Roll out the top of the pie in exactly the same fashion as before. Load the rolling pin with pastry and unfurl the pastry neatly over the pie and filling.

Secure the edge of the top pastry onto the edge of the bottom pastry by just pressing down, then using a pinching motion – pinch and move, pinch and move – leaving a lovely pinched and secure edge.

Set the oven at 160°C.

Only now are we going to trim the edge. With the pie held up in your non-dominant hand, take the sharp knife in your dominant hand and offer it up to the edge of the pie. You're looking to cut the edge, but at a 45° angle. Keep the inside edge of the knife touching the pie dish and with an up-and-down motion with the knife hand, whilst turning the pie dish at the same time, slice off the rough edges at a 45° angle, so that the pastry when it shrinks doesn't shrink too far.

Egg-wash the pie and push three slits in the very middle of the top to help the pie breathe whilst cooking. Cook for 40 minutes with a baking sheet at the bottom of the oven to catch any juices. If the top is golden way before 40 minutes, cover with foil and continue to cook. Take off the foil with 4 minutes to go.

You should now have a lava-hot apple pie. Please leave it to cool for 15 minutes before even attempting to dive in!

The pie crust will have a lovely, Cheddary, cidery flavour, and the chunky Cheddar in the filling will have melted, giving a lovely, Cheddary, appley flavour.

Englishness on a plate ...

APPLE, FRANGIPANE AND CHEDDAR STRUDEL – WITH HOMEMADE VIENNESE PHYLLO PASTRY (V)

SERVES 6

The creation of great patisserie is one of my loves and it is this love that has brought many happy hours in the kitchen. This Viennese strudel could be made with shop-bought filo pastry, but here I am making an authentic version with traditional phyllo pastry from Vienna – a great skill to have under your belt if you're a proper home cook/baker. The additions I have made here are twofold: I've added my favourite, frangipane, and then added a strong, vintage Cheddar. These two additions make, what we know as the ultimate strudel, the living end in desserts. Accompanied with a vanilla/Cheddar ice cream would blow the top off any dessert menu. The only regret I have is that NO restaurant would attempt this dessert and so you have me here to guide you through this gorgeous recipe. The difficulty level is quite high, but as I say, you can always substitute with shop-bought filo – which I have done on many cooking demonstrations, and it works a treat. I have a clever way of 'cradling' the strudel in the baking tray that makes for a great shape too.

EQUIPMENT:

Medium-sized, heavy-based pan

Container for the raisins

Mixing bowl

Liquidiser or hand blitzer

34x24cm roasting tray

2lb loaf tin

Clean tea towel

Greaseproof paper

Scissors

FRANGIPANE

65g butter
100g ground almonds
70g sugar

½–¾ tsp almond essence
1 egg

METHOD

Melt your butter in a deep based pan. Add the almonds and sugar and mix to combine. Add the almond essence and take off the heat, then add the egg and thoroughly mix to combine.

Decant into a dessert bowl and refrigerate for 1 hour.

PHYLLO DOUGH

80ml warm water
1 tbsp oil
½ tsp vinegar to soften glutens
⅛ tsp salt

Deep bowl to mix
Wooden spoon
145g bread flour
Flour to dust work surface

METHOD

Put the water, vinegar, salt and oil into the bowl and add half the flour. Mix to a creamy finish and then add the rest of the flour.

Bring into a dough ball and start kneading for 10 minutes, adding lightly dusted flour as needed. You need a tacky dough, but not sticky. Once you get here throw (hard) your dough onto the work surface repeatedly (10 times) to help with the glutens.

Leave in a dessert bowl with half a teaspoon of oil rubbed around and covered.

BREADCRUMBS

120g crustless sourdough
  (preferable but not essential)
  breadcrumbs

60g butter
50g sugar
A good few shakes of cinnamon

METHOD

Melt the butter in a frying pan and add the breadcrumbs. Keep the crumb moving with the wooden spoon and bring up in heat to begin colouring the crumb. Cook further until golden and crunchy and take off the heat. Add sugar and cinnamon and decant into a bowl. Set aside.

FILLING ASSEMBLY

EQUIPMENT:
Frying pan
Mixing bowl

APPLES:
2 Gala apples or similar
A scant tsp of cinnamon
Juice of half a lemon

METHOD

Halve and core the apples, then quarter them and add the lemon juice and cinnamon. Set aside.

SULTANAS:

4 tbsp sultanas in a bowl

3 tbsp rum

Combine and steep for an hour.

CHEDDAR:

Grate 100g of mature Cheddar. Set aside.

You will need a deep-sided baking tray, a prepared 2lb loaf tin, and a small pan with 60g of melted butter.

Set the oven to 180°C. Have a cup of tea and carefully read the assembly.

STRUDEL ASSEMBLY:

This could be like the *Generation Game* so read this more than once before attempting.

With a fresh tea towel on a work surface, cut greaseproof/baking paper to fit tea towel. Butter the paper well.

Flour your work surface (next to the towel) and begin rolling out the pastry to approximately 15x13in with a 3mm thickness.

Take off all jewellery.

Pick up the pastry by one edge with both hands at a 12 o'clock position.

Place the back of your hands (cupped) into the top (12 o'clock) of your hanging circle of dough, so your palms are facing you and the dough is hanging off the back of your hands.

Begin passing the edge of the dough from cupped hand to cupped hand, so the motion turns the circle of dough clockwise.

Start carefully and slowly.

You will notice the pastry stretching as you go.

Don't panic at this stage – just keep going in the same motion, passing the dough from hand to hand. If you get a hole in the dough all is not lost, but be careful.

Keep going until the stretch becomes nearly see-through and roughly about the size of your tea towel.

Carefully lay down the stretched dough onto the buttered parchment and begin stretching by hand to cover the parchment practically fully.

Trim off the thicker edges all around into a neat rectangle.

If you have a hole this is where you refill the excess and stretch in the same fashion as before and then repair the hole.

Brush melted butter all over the surface of the dough.

Making sure the short side of the tea towel is nearest you – you should have a rectangle of dough with short sides top and bottom – just slide the tea towel on the work surface.

Now for the filling:

Evenly spread the top half with crispy breadcrumbs.

4 inches down from the top lay a line of (sticky) frangipane 2 inches wide from left to right.

Push and stack the apples into the frangipane to start building your strudel. Cover all the frangipane with apple (left to right).

Sprinkle over sultanas.

Sprinkle the grated cheese over the strudel filling from left to right.

You need to take a deep breath here.

And relax!

We are now going to roll the strudel, from top (furthest away edge) to bottom (nearest edge).

Carefully lift the parchment at the top edge and peel away the pastry from the parchment to roughly half cover the strudel.

Carefully fold over the side edges 2 inches all the way down both sides, to tuck in the two ends of the strudel.

With the parchment in both hands start lifting the parchment and with the flat of your best hand tease away the dough at the same time to start covering the strudel, whilst lifting and rolling (all at the same time!). It's a knack so be slow and careful.

You should have a cylinder of strudel with the two ends nicely tucked in at the bottom of the towel and nearest to you.

At this point you can (carefully) use your hands to manoeuvre the strudel into its cylinder shape.

Phew!

Paint with melted butter and sprinkle sugar and shake some cinnamon over the top, sparingly.

You are now looking to cradle the strudel in the middle of your parchment, by sliding the strudel carefully up to the middle, leaving the same amount of parchment top and bottom, thus creating the cradle.

Now fold down the top and bottom edge of the parchment to re-enforce the cradle of parchment.

This cradle of strudel will now be lifted and placed into the roasting tray, touching one long edge of the tray. Carefully place the loaf tin on the tray to snugly fit up to the other edge to support the strudel so that both edges are supported.

Place into the middle of your oven for 30 minutes or until golden.

Once out of the oven, carefully lift out the cradle of strudel and place directly onto a cutting board to rest for 5 minutes.

You now have a traditional Viennese strudel with Cheddar cheese.

Slice and present in dessert bowls topped with vanilla ice cream.

Easy!

EXTRA SHORT CHEESE BISCUITS (V)

MAKES 14

The question of biscuits and crackers always comes up when people know I'm around – it's an answer that most people want to know. These short biscuits are simply sublime to whip out of the larder to impress friends, but they're quite something straight from the oven too. It's a simple biscuit really, but scratch biscuits are a dying art. It's the shortness and cheesiness that carries this great recipe over the line. Make sure you keep them in an airtight container too, as you need to capture that shortness at its best. Of course the quality of the Cheddar will show itself in this recipe too. I use Wyke Farms' 'Ivy's Vintage' which just gets the ache in the tonsils going every time – you know the ache!

A great soft cheese or a clothbound Cheddar laid on top of this biscuit will have you in raptures of delight.

On the question of which cracker I prefer for cheese, my tip would be 'Matso's', the high-bake, no-salt cracker, available in most supermarkets. Because there is no salt, they allow you to taste the real flavour of the cheese. Once experienced, never forgotten!

EQUIPMENT:
Mixing bowl
Grater
2 baking sheets
Fork
Sieve

INGREDIENTS:
120g plain flour – sifted
60g unsalted butter – softened
60g Cheddar – grated (vintage is best, but leftover Cheddar will suffice)
Pinch of salt
Freshly ground black pepper
1 egg yolk
1–2 tbsp cider

METHOD:

First sift the flour into your mixing bowl and then add the softened butter and the cheese. By lifting and rubbing the butter in your fingers you will eventually have the appearance of breadcrumbs in your bowl. Add the salt and pepper and mix. Make a hole in the middle of your mixture and then add the egg yolk and the cider. Carefully mix to combine. If you need more cider, add very carefully. You want the dough to be not too wet, but not too dry either – so it just keeps together without falling apart.

Flour your baking sheets in readiness for the biscuits.

Flour your work surface and knead the dough briefly.

Roll out the dough to 5mm depth and cut out your biscuits carefully and transport them over to the baking sheets. With your fork you will need to carefully prick the surface of each biscuit. Slide the baking sheets into the oven – just make sure the biscuits are not too close to each other as they will spread a little in the oven.

Cook in the middle of your pre-heated oven for 9–12 minutes or until golden brown.

Cool on a rack.

Cheesetastic!

CHEDDAR CHEERS!

*May your Cheddar experience
always be better because of this book.*

If you want to become a 'Cheesemeister' just join my social media

 @seanwilsonchef   seancheese   @Sean6809